"It's a wonderful outline of the new anti-capitalist activity... It pulls together all aspects of changes to all levels of education, as it is drawn into the profit business – and ever further away from wider concepts of education."

Caroline Benn, Hillcole Group; President of the Socialist Education Association

"This is essential reading for all those the world over who have been driven to the margins of existence by forces of the current phase of capitalism – globalisation. It helps to understand the forces hiding behind bodies such as the World Trade Organisation that drive us relentlessly towards giving up control over our minds and bodies. It also shows that people's resistance can make a difference in snatching control over their lives."

Shiraz Durrani, Information for Social Change

"Glenn Rikowski vividly demonstrates the centrality of education in capitalist globalisation. Rikowski's seminal text is destined to become essential reading for critical/radical educators and political activists, but it should be read by everyone who is concerned with, and about, the future of education... indeed, the future of humanity."

Paula Allman, Honorary Research Fellow, University of Nottingham

"Glenn Rikowski has produced a brilliant and I believe historical landmark in Left education."

Peter McLaren, University of California, Los Angeles,

"I felt compelled to grab the red flag and take to the streets as I worked through Glenn Rikowski's well documented *exposé* of what the World Trade Organisation is up to and its plans for education. But Glenn's analysis is much more than a clarion call. It anchors that call in solid theory and critique so that my immediate response can now be matched by informed and focused action. An activist's true handbook."

Helen Raduntz, University of South Australia

the Hillcole Group

The Hillcole Group is a group of Radical Left Educators, formed in 1989 with three aims:

1) To influence policy and decision making on educational matters;

2) To respond rapidly to assaults on the quality of education from the Radical Right;

3) To improve the quality of schooling and of teacher education.

As a writing group, we have been producing a continuous series of publications in pursuit of the above aims. Our earlier books have been critiques of the Radical Right and the way in which their theories and policies have affected schooling, further education and teacher education.

Collective Hillcole publications represent the views of the Hillcole Group as a whole. Singly or co-authored publications do not necessarily reflect the views of every individual Hillcole member. As we are a writing collective, all Hillcole publications are subject to comments on and are discussed by the Group.

The Battle in Seattle
its significance for education

Glenn Rikowski

the Tufnell Press

the Tufnell Press,
47 Dalmeny Road,
London, N7 0DY

Copyright © 2001, Glenn Rikowski

First published 2001

British Library Cataloguing-in-Publication Data
A catalogue record for this book is
available from the British Library

ISBN 1 872767 370

Printed in England by Da Costa Print, London

Contents

Glenn Rikowski is Senior Research Fellow in Lifelong Learning, Faculty of Education, University of Central England in Birmingham, UK. He has been a member of the Hillcole Group of Radical Left Educators since 1994.

PREFACE

The Morning after Prague

The mass media discovered a new phrase in 1999—'anti-capitalism' ...They were painfully discovering something very real. Ten years after the supposed final triumph of market capitalism with the fall of the Berlin Wall and the collapse of the USSR, a growing number of people were rejecting their system (Chris Harman, *Anti-capitalism: theory and practice*, 2000, p. 3).

World trade is the mechanism allowing poor countries to start taking care of very basic needs. (Bill Gates, in Barkham, 2000).

UPDATE 19:50 (26th September 2000, Prague): The Opera has been cancelled due to 'unforeseen circumstances.' ...UPDATE 19:39 Delegates [of the IMF and World Bank] are going to the Opera Square where a big party is waiting for them, but three thousand protestors are already in the square. ...UPDATE (from Tel-Aviv): Reports of a completely successful shutdown of down-town Tel-Aviv are coming in. Demonstrators totally took over a square and held a moment of silence in solidarity with actions in Praha. ...UPDATE 18:43: Reports of mass arrests have begun. ...UPDATE 15:27: Demonstrators have broken through police lines around the convention center. More than 500 are directly outside the convention center. ...UPDATE 13:20: Reports of massive police violence from under the bridge to the convention center. Gas, spray, water cannons and other weapons are being used against people marching toward the convention center from the valley ... (Nasreen Karim, *Fighting back in Prague*, extracts of eyewitness report from Prague, PSN, 27th September: 00. 52).

The idea for a pamphlet on the significance of Seattle for education was first discussed at a Hillcole Group meeting held in February, 2000. For us, as radical left educators, it seemed that Seattle was a significant landmark regarding the struggle against reducing education to labour-power production, against the insertion of business interests into all sectors of education (schools, colleges, universities) and against privatisation of education. It became increasingly

apparent—especially after the groundbreaking work of Nico Hirtt (2000)—
that the World Trade Organisation (WTO) through its Council for Trade in
Services (CTS) was softening education up as a site for corporate competition.
The 'businessification' of education (Benn and Chitty, 1999) that we discussed
in our *Business, Business, Business: New Labour's Education Policy* (Allen *et
al*, 1999) and at our Conference (of the same title) held in London in October
1999, clearly had a *global* dimension. Education was just another profit-making
site, to be opened up to international capital by the WTO's Council for Services.
This pamphlet uncovers the WTO's neo-liberal agenda for education.

The text of the pamphlet started life as the first three sections of a paper
written for the Annual Conference of Socialist Economists 2000, 'Global
Capital and Global Struggles: strategies, alliances, alternatives', held at the
University of London Union in July (Rikowski, 2000a). Section 4 owes a lot
to two papers presented at the recent British Educational Research Association
Annual Conference, Cardiff University, in September (Rikowski, 2000b, c).
Further, this pamphlet incorporates ideas and discussions from a number of
Hillcole Group publications (especially Chitty, 1991; Hillcole Group, 1997;
Allen *et al*, 1999; and Hill, 1999), and from our meetings.

Seattle was not the first protest against one or more of the triad of
organisations policing the world for international capital—the International
Monetary Fund (IMF), the World Bank and the WTO. Peter McLaren (2000,
p.26) points to the Second Ministerial Meeting in Geneva 1998, where 10,000
anti-WTO protestors were in evidence. Neither was Seattle the first
recognisably 'anti-capitalist' mass protest (London's Carnival Against Capital,
of 18th June 1999, holds that honour). Yet Seattle was the biggest mass protest
against one of the triad organisations, and, furthermore, for a significant number
of the protestors, it was simultaneously *against capitalism* as a way of life.
Seattle has, of course, been followed by Davos (World Economic Forum),
Washington, May Day 2000, Melbourne and other protests against the triad
organisations, or against what they stand for: the penetration of international
capital into all areas of social life, neo-liberalism, and subservience to the law
of money.

The Prague protest against the IMF and the World Bank going on at the
time of writing is the latest in the line—and will not be the last. In a world
where 7 million children die each year as a result of their country's debt burden
(Mayor of London, Ken Livingstone, in Thomas, 2000), the complacency and
pro-capitalist policies of the leading capitalist powers cannot be tolerated. In a
world where every £1 given in Western aid to developing countries is matched
by £13 returning to the creditor nations to service debt (*ibid.*), the anger that
fuels anti-capitalist protests will continue. Seeing the writing on the wall,
business may try to co-opt radical opponents; valuing them precisely for their

capacity to change public opinion (see Unilever's pathetic attempt to woo activist Naomi Klein, in Heur, 2000).

Eyewitness accounts from Prague (e.g. Karim, 2000) suggest that the mainstream media are seriously under-reporting what is happening there. It is clear that the media do not want to credit the protestors with any indication of success. On the contrary, Prague is being presented in the UK media as a tiresome, violent yet basically insignificant affair (as in reports by Anderson, 2000; and Huggler, 2000). In *The Times*, Prague is tucked away in a small article on page 19, with a single picture of two people in a cloud of tear gas (Paterson, 2000). The message seems to be 'this is not important, it's violent and unpleasant and these protestors are very sad people'—but even *The Times* cannot entirely hide the significance of Prague or the courage of the protestors. The mask slips in an article by Simon Jenkins reporting on Prime Minister Tony Blair's speech at the Labour Party Conference in Brighton yesterday (Jenkins, 2000). Near the end of the article, Jenkins notes that:

> Politics in the last quarter of the 20th century has rid domestic government of any need for moral crusade. This may be no bad thing. But oh, the dullness of it all. The longer I listened to Mr Blair, the more I yearned to pack my rucksack and head for Wenceslas Square. There was the cockpit of the last modern revolution. There now is the cauldron of global change. It is in Prague, not in London or Brighton, that 10,000 policemen must protect the new supranational politicians, with their grants, backhanders, consultancies and construction rackets. There I could see myself smashing a few windows and grabbing a helmet or two. There is where the poor need a voice and the downtrodden a revolution. Forget Brighton.

The future will bring greater thrills than even Simon Jenkins can stand, though from the above I suspect that when pushed by a tide of solid and substantial victories for social transformation his penchant for dullness in life may win out.

Some elements within the mainstream media have presented possibilities for protest in Prague as a nuisance for the Czech people, using divide-and-rule formulas. Today, the UK press seems keen to remind us that many of Prague's inhabitants have simply fled the city (e.g. Anderson, 2000). An article in *Newsweek* argued that many young Eastern Europeans support globalisation and the 'cool' products and riches it promises (Lowry Miller, 2000). However, Sam Ashman (2000, p.8) shows that 20% unemployment in parts of Bohemia and eastern Moravia takes the shine off globalisation for many Czechs. A recently announced 43% increase in electricity prices, 27% increase in rents, the exploitation of cheap labour, poverty and racism (especially against the Roma) indicate global capital is likely to bring benefits only to segments of the business and professional classes.

For radical Left educators, the transference of the magic of struggle against social injustice from Seattle to Prague forces us once more to rethink the role, nature and place of education within the mad social universe of capital. On the WTO's agenda for education uncovered in this pamphlet, it seems that education institutions, education research (increasingly becoming a dull appendage of the Labour administration's Department for Education and Employment) and education policy have lost their innocence. They are now part of a programme for incorporating all spheres of social life within the orbit of global capital. Educators are implicated in this process, like everyone else. The school or university is no hiding place.

The key point is what we do about it. The Battle in Seattle and its subsequent incarnations are reminders that educators are never off the hook until the need for further Seattles has been eradicated.

Glenn Rikowski
Birmingham, 27th September, 2000

References

Allen, M. , Benn, C. , Chitty, C. , Cole, M. , Hatcher, R. , Hirtt, N. & Rikowski, G. (1999) *Business, Business, Business: New Labour's Education Policy*. A Hillcole Paper (London: Tufnell Press).

Anderson, R. (2000) Police halt violent march on conference centre. *Financial Times*, 27th September: 18.

Ashman, S. (2000) The Czech Republic: 10 Years of Free Market Disaster. *Socialist Worker*, 23rd September: 8-9.

Barkham, P. (2000) Gates rounds on protestors. *The Guardian (e-finance)*, 13th September: 24.

Benn, C. & Chitty, C. (1999) Conclusion: There is an alternative, in: M. Allen, C. Benn, C. Chitty, M. Cole, R. Hatcher, N. Hirtt & G. Rikowski (1999) *Business, Business, Business: New Labour's Education Policy*, A Hillcole Paper (London: Tufnell Press).

Harman, C. (2000) Anti-capitalism: theory and practice. *International Socialism*, September, no. 88: 3-59.

Heur, S. (2000) Six Degrees of Co-Optation. *The Industry Standard: The Newsmagazine of the Internet Economy*, 3rd July, 3(25): 196-199.

Hill, D. (1999) *New Labour and Education: Policy, Ideology and the Third Way*. A Hillcole Paper (London: Tufnell Press).

Hillcole Group (1997) *Rethinking Education and Democracy: A Socialist Alternative for the Twenty-first Century* (London: Tufnell Press).

Hirtt, N. (2000) The 'Millennium Round' and the Liberalisation of the Education Market. *Education and Social Justice*, 2(2): 12-18.

Huggler, J. (2000) The banners proclaimed non-violence but Molotov cocktails were at the ready. *The Independent*, 27th September: 2.

Jenkins, S. (2000) Whatever happened to Labour's passion? *The Times*, 27th September: 22.

Lowry Miller, K. (2000) East Loves West. *Newsweek*, 5th September, CXXXVI(13): 30-36.

Karim, N. (2000) *Fighting back in Prague*. Eyewitness account distributed through the Progressive Sociologists Network, 27th September (2 pages) at: prague.indymedia.org/breaking_news. php3

McLaren, P. (2000) *Che Guevara, Paulo Freire, and the Pedagogy of Revolution* (Lanham, ML: Rowman & Littlefield).

The battle in Seattle: Its significance for education

Ladies and gentlemen: This conference is doomed—doomed to succeed. (Opening Address to the WTO's 3rd Ministerial Conference in Seattle by Mike Moore, WTO Director-General, WTO, 1999b, p.2)

Seattle ... will signal the kind of world we can expect in the new century. (Mike Moore, WTO, 2000, p.1)

November 30 is a date that will be etched into American history. It was a day that saw the US president flying into a city in his own country under martial law, in a state of civil emergency. It was a day which began with the biggest protests in the USA since Vietnam and ended with the first curfew in Seattle since WWII. It was the day civil society challenged corporate power—and won (Gibby Zobel, 1999, p.14)

The great demonstrations in Seattle will make its reverberations felt for years to come. (Alex Callinicos, 1999)

There's something in the air; a new mode of radical activism of a kind—and perhaps—scale not seen for years. (Michael Elliott, 1999, p.27)

The greatest victory of the Battle of Seattle is that it has transformed how people see themselves. ... After Seattle the term 'anti-capitalist' is a commonplace of astounded journalists and news readers ... (John Rees, 2000, p.9)

Introduction

Why did over 40, 000 people demonstrate against the World Trade Organisation (WTO) in Seattle in late 1999? What do struggles against transnational institutions such as the WTO have to do with what goes on in education? What is the significance of education for production in today's global capitalism and for post-Seattle political strategies? These are the questions at the heart of this pamphlet.

The argument is presented two-fold: on the one hand the pamphlet explores the significance of the Battle in Seattle for education, and on the other the significance of education for anti-capitalist struggles post-Seattle. On the first count, it examines the WTO's forays into education as part of its expanding influence through its Council for Trade in Services (CTS). This illustrates the *direct* significance of the Battle in Seattle for education. On the second count, the argument has two aspects. First, education is intimately involved in the

social production of the one commodity upon which contemporary capitalist
society depends; that is human *labour-power* (the capacity to labour), which
takes the form of 'human capital' in contemporary society. Second, and related
to this first point, is that education can potentially become a site of struggle
and strategic engagement for the establishment of principles for critical and
socialist pedagogies. Examples of such principles were provided in the Hillcole
Group's *Rethinking Education and Democracy* (of 1997).

In all the post-Seattle debates on socialist grand strategy and the grittier
problems surrounding 'what is to be done' next, education has not figured
greatly. This pamphlet seeks to remedy the situation by arguing that education
has a central role to play in the struggles ahead. This is demonstrated in the
following way. The first section provides a brief history of the development of
the WTO up to the Battle in Seattle of late 1999—providing background and
detail for those requiring key elements of the plot and setting the scene for
those familiar with the main events. Section 2 outlines some of political debates
and issues flowing from the events in Seattle and argues the need for 'socialist
vision' in thinking and struggling our way through towards socialism after
Seattle. A section linking directly the Battle in Seattle with developments in
education today follows this. It shows how education was a core element of
the Seattle agenda. The fourth section approaches the question of the
significance of Seattle for education from the opposite direction by asking a
more general question: what is the significance of education for capitalist
production? Based on an exploration of pertinent ideas within the works of
Karl Marx, it is argued that education and training in capitalism are elements
within processes that constitute the social production of labour-power in
capitalism. As labour-power is the unique commodity, upon which the whole
capitalist production system rests, the significance of education is uncovered.
This section explores how the WTO's agenda for education is likely to impact
on the social production of labour-power. The Conclusion poses the questions
of *alternatives* to education and training as institutions involved in reducing
humanity to labour-power. Drawing upon earlier work from the Hillcole Group
(especially Hillcole Group, 1997; and Allen *et al*, 1999), the roles of critical
pedagogies and principles for educational and societal transformation are
examined. As Caroline Benn and Clyde Chitty argue in their contribution to
Hillcole's *Business, Business, Business: New Labour's Education Policy* (Allen
et al, 1999):

> Every time we criticise changes being made, we must suggest what
> changes are required instead. It is much harder to do this but that is what
> the Hillcole Group was formed to do. (Benn and Chitty, 1999, p.39)

1. The World Trade Organisation and the Battle in Seattle

Whilst the Second World War was still raging, in 1943 the US and British governments embarked on a series of bilateral discussions aimed at designing a post-War international trading system free of the protectionism of the inter-War years (Cohn, 2000, p.205). In the autumn of 1945, the US State Department floated a document on trade and employment that was to be the basis of multilateral negotiations. It constituted an outline for a proposed International Trade Organisation (ITO). This document was developed as the basis for the Havana Charter that was discussed by 23 leading capitalist countries in March 1948. Meanwhile, in 1946, the same 23 nations met to discuss the much narrower issue of tariff reduction. At this meeting it was decided to meet up the following year in Geneva to negotiate to reduce tariffs on about a fifth of the world's trade. Thus, in October 1947 the first round of the General Agreement on Tariffs and Trade (GATT) resulted in these 23 countries signing up to the agreement, which became effective on 1st January 1948 (MSN Encarta, 2000a). Furthermore, the signatories agreed to accept some of the trade rules enshrined within the draft ITO charter (ahead of the forthcoming meeting in Havana) in order to protect the tariff reductions negotiated in Geneva.

Thus, the GATT emerged after the Second World War as a charter for the ITO, which was envisioned as an agency of the United Nations (MSN Encarta, 2000a). The ITO was to complement the World Bank and the International Monetary Fund in establishing international trade rules and co-operation (DTI, 1999b, p.1). However, it was at the meeting in Havana in March 1948 that this broader scenario started to unravel. The main aim of the meeting was to attain agreement to the formation of a permanent ITO. The 1947 GATT agreement was to be incorporated within the ITO. The ITO charter was to have had 'an ambitious agenda' (DTI, 1999b, p.1). It was to cover not just trading relations but also employment, international investment, economic development, services, competition, restrictive practices and commercial policy and commodity agreements. It also included the administrative arrangements for a permanent ITO (Penrose, 1953; Reisman, 1996; DTI, 1999b; Cohn, 2000). As Tabb noted:

> The ITO was to impose order on the world trading system, in order to avoid the kind of protectionist downward spiral in trade which occurred in the 1930s. (2000a, p.4)

The ITO was not ratified at Havana (or thereafter). Cohn (2000, p.205-206) presents the ITO as a dog's breakfast, with complex rules and 'numerous escape clauses and exceptions in the charter [that] would interfere with trade liberalization' (p. 205). He also noted the disruptive effects for the ITO charter of the strong US protectionist lobby (*ibid.*). Yet Tabb (2000a) argues that it was the possibility of the ITO providing substantive protection on labour standards and meeting the needs of developing countries that effectively sank it. From a United States' perspective, the ITO framework for regulating international trade yielded too much to workers' rights and Third World countries' yearnings for preferential treatment in trade, and set too tight a leash on big corporations' market power (promising anti-trust laws) (Tabb, 2000a, p.4-5). On this score, the United States dragged its heels over ratifying the ITO. In 1950, the ITO failed to win ratification in the US Congress and was consigned to history. The GATT, meanwhile, remained in use to regulate international trade.

From its 'provisional' status as precursor to the ITO in 1948, the GATT provided a legal and institutional framework for international trade and tariffs to 1995 (DTI, 1999b). Its participants were 'contracting parties' rather than members; the GATT was never formally constituted. It aimed at non-discrimination in the sense that all participants were to be treated equally, such that when a country reduced trade tariffs for one GATT participant it had to do so for all. Secondly, there was a clause that enabled a GATT participant to withdraw its tariff reduction if it 'seriously harmed' its domestic producers (MSN Encarta, 2000a). This was a loophole that GATT participants were keen to exploit, pointing towards a need for a more formal trade dispute mechanism. The GATT participants sponsored eight 'trade rounds' in all. The 'Kennedy Round' (1962-67) established a set of trade negotiation rules when parties disagreed. The Tokyo Round (1973-79) established a series of non-tariff barrier codes of practice in the areas of government procurement, customs valuation, subsidies and countervailing measures, anti-dumping, standards and import licensing (Antweiler, 1995).

The final 'Uruguay Round' (1986-94) broadened the GATT agreement further by limiting agricultural subsidies and including trade in services and intellectual property within its scope. This round also established the World Trade Organisation (WTO). The GATT and the WTO co-existed throughout 1995, and the former was wound up in December 1995. Trade agreements established by the GATT became incorporated within the WTO agreement (MSN Encarta, 2000b). In 1995, GATT's functions were taken over by the WTO.

The WTO is based permanently in Geneva and is controlled by a General Council comprising member states' ambassadors (who also serve on WTO committees) (*ibid.*). The Ministerial Conference meets every two years, and appoints the WTO's Director-General (currently Mike Moore). It has a budget of £48m and 500 staff (Legrain, 2000, p.30). The Seattle meeting in 1999 was the 3rd Ministerial Conference. There are 135 member countries, and a further 35 nations have observer status. China is currently negotiating to be the 136th.[1]

As Bakan (2000a, p.22-23) has noted, the WTO extends far the remit of the old GATT. It includes a series of other agreements:

- Trade Related Investment Measures (TRIMS);
- Trade Related Intellectual Property Measures (TRIPS);
- General Agreement on Trade in Services (GATS);
- Sanitary and Phyto-sanitary Standards Agreement (SPS) (setting restrictive standards on government policies regarding food and safety and animal and plant health);
- Financial Services Agreement (FSA)—designed to remove all obstacles to financial services.
- Agreements on agriculture, information technology and telecommunications.

Furthermore, the WTO incorporates a complex Dispute Settlement Process. Tribunals operate in secret to settle disputes between member states. Only national governments are allowed to participate, and there is no outside appeals procedure (Working Group on the WTO/MAI, 1999, p.5). Rulings generate three possibilities. First, losing countries have a set time to comply and they must change their laws to conform to WTO stipulations. Secondly, if they refuse to do this then they pay *permanent* compensation to the winning country. The third possibility is that they face non-negotiated trade sanctions (*ibid.*). As Smith and Moran (2000, p.66) have noted:

> What distinguishes the WTO among international agreements is its Dispute Resolution Panel. The panel possesses far-reaching sanctioning powers over member countries, which it uses to ensure compliance with WTO commitments. No other international body has such strong enforcement capabilities.

The WTO is 'the only global institution that even the US and the EU are supposed to obey', whereas the World Bank and the International Monetary Fund have influence only over 'weak developing countries', notes Martin Wolf (1999), a journalist for the *Financial Times*.

On disputes other than trade, the WTO operates on a system of 'consensus', but in practice this process is driven by the 'Quad'—the US, the EU, Japan and Canada—whose representatives meet daily in Geneva to address these non-trade issues (Bakan, 2000a, p.23). Representatives from the 'Quad' are lobbied heavily by transnational corporations. Furthermore, representatives from transnational corporations 'sit on all the important advisory committees' deciding detailed policy and set the agenda (Price, Pollock and Shaoul, 1999: 1889). Thus, the WTO provides an 'enforceable global commercial code' based on close relations with transnational capital, making it 'one of the main mechanisms of corporate globalization' (Working Group on the WTO/MAI, 1999, p.1). It is a 'forum for trade rights of capital, on terms negotiated by the agencies of governments that represent the interests of capital. No other rights count' (Tabb, 2000a, p.6). Trade barriers are essentially '*anything* that can limit profits made via trade or investment' (Puckett, 2000).

The outlook underpinning the WTO is deregulation, with incremental 'freedom for transnational capital to do what it wants, where and when it wants' (Tabb, 2000a, p.5). As Tabb has noted, the 'WTO's fundamental postulate is that trade and investment liberalization lead to more competition, greater market efficiency and so, necessarily, to a higher standard of living' (*ibid.*).[2] These principles and propositions are the essence of the concept of 'neo-liberalism' in the international economy. However:

> While its proponents say it is based on 'free trade', in fact, the WTO's 700-plus pages of rules set out a comprehensive system of *corporate-managed trade*. Under the WTO's system of corporate-managed trade, economic efficiency, reflected in short-term corporate profits, dominates other values. The neoliberal ideological underpinning of corporate-managed trade is presented as TINA—'There Is No Alternative'—an inevitable outcome rather than the culmination of a long-term effort to write and put in place rules designed to benefit corporations and investors, rather than communities, workers and the environment. (Working Group on the WTO/MAI, p.1—original emphasis)

BOX 1: Neo-liberalism

National focus
1) inflation should be controlled by interest rates, preferably by an independent central bank
2) budgets should be balanced and not used to influence demand - or at any rate not to stimulate it
3) unemployment is solely a problem of the labour market

International focus
1) barriers to international trade and capitalist enterprise should be removed

> 2) there should be a 'level playing field' for companies of any nationality within all sectors of national economies
>
> 3) trade rules and regulations are necessary to underpin 'free' trade, with a system for penalising 'unfair' trade practices
>
> Adapted from Ainley (1999: 161)

The anger directed at the WTO's 3ʳᵈ Ministerial meeting in Seattle late November—early December 1999 was underwritten by over fifty years of capital-friendly developments in organisational changes in the international trading infrastructure. Yet Seattle is an instant within a series of acts of resistance to global capital. These incorporate landless peasants (NST) movements in Brazil, Mexico's Zapatistas, the farmers of India's Karnataka state, a 50,000 strong demonstration in the Niger Delta, Jubilee 2000, the J18 Carnival Against Capitalism in London and more besides (Bakan, 2000a; Madden, 2000). The spirit of Seattle has been continued by the Davos (Switzerland, World Economic Forum meeting) demonstration and the May Day resistances in London and many other cities across the world. Peter McLaren (2000, p.26) reminds us that 10, 000 protestors picketed the WTO's Second Ministerial Meeting in Geneva in May 1998. Ward and Wadsworth argue that: 'Seattle was not the beginning, but the result of many small to medium movements that have been gathering strength for over two years' (2000, p.4).

The Seattle Ministerial was set up to produce an agenda for the next 'Millennial Round' of negotiations. When the 'Millennial Round' opened in Seattle on 30ᵗʰ November 1999, the ministers and delegates were confronted by 40, 000 anti-WTO protestors, which was more than the '20-30,000 that shut down Interstate 5 to protest about the Vietnam War' (Tabb, 2000a, p.1). The protestors represented around 800 trade union and activist organisations from more than seventy-five countries (Tabb, 2000a, p.2). The vibrancy, creativity and courage that they incorporated into their strategies for shutting down the Seattle ministerial were stunning.[3] Despite being shot at with rubber bullets, tear-gassed and pepper sprayed the mass of protestors prevented ministers and the WTO *entourage* from addressing their agenda; they 'left Seattle in disarray' (Bakan, 2000a, p.19). Mazur (2000, p.93) argues that the anger expressed in Seattle resulted from developments in the world economy failing to benefit labour as against capital and these changes (summed up by the concept of 'globalisation') had not been accompanied by new democratic organisations giving ordinary people a voice on these developments. But this position ignores the fact that Seattle was an alliance of organised labour with a myriad of social movements, grassroots organisations and environmental groups (as illustrated in Charlton (2000), and in the video *Showdown in Seattle*—see fn. 3).

As some (Mandel and Magnussen, 1999) have noted, the limited discussions that did take place merely showed up serious rifts within the WTO as some Third World countries set out to block proposals for the next trade round. Furthermore, some countries made pledges to 'free trade' whilst lobbying seriously for rules favourable to their own economies (Mandel and Magnussen, 1999, p.39). Finally, Marshall (1999) points towards familiar EU/US splits in Seattle. Even without the demonstrators it would have been no picnic.

BOX 2: Globalisation

• The increasing importance and significance of the financial structure and the global creation of credit, leading to the dominance of finance over production.

• The growing importance of the 'knowledge structure': knowledge is said to have become a significant factor of production.

• The increase in the rapidity of redundancy of technologies and the increase in the transnationalisation of technology: an emphasis on knowledge-based industries with increasing reliance on technological innovation.

• The rise of global oligopolies in the form of multinational corporations: corporations appear to have no choice but to 'go global', and multinational corporations and transnational banks have become the significant power centres beyond national states and economies.

• The globalisation of production, knowledge and finance is viewed to have led to a decline in the regulative power of national states. This is accompanied by the rise of global authority structures - such as the United Nations, the G7 (now G8) group of industrial powers and the WTO, International Monetary Fund (IMF) and World Bank.

• The 'new freedom' of capital from national regulative control and democratic accountability is held to have lead to increased ecological destruction, social fragmentation and poverty - as well as having effects for personal identity as global media corporations homogenise, customise and niche market their products.

(Adapted from Bonefeld, 1999, p. 76-77)

In the aftermath, the WTO was frantically spinning the story that the negotiations that had taken place in Seattle were enough for the Geneva office to work up firm proposals for the next trade round in January 2000.[4] Smith and Moran (2000, p.66) indicated cautiously that the 'Millennium Round' was 'temporarily derailed', whilst *The Economist* announced bleakly that:

... sectoral negotiations on agriculture and services, which WTO members will start in Geneva in January, are unlikely to make any progress. Their prospects are clouded by the lack of agreed objectives or deadlines ... (Economist, 1999c, p.21)

Lacayo (1999, p.37) was in no doubt that:

... the [WTO] bureaucrats may not have accomplished all that much last week. The chaos that surrounded them did. In this moment of triumphant capitalism, of planetary cash flows and a priapic Dow, all the second thoughts and outright furies about the global economy collected on the streets of downtown Seattle and crashed through the windows of Nike Town. After two days of uproar scented with tear gas and pepper spray, the world may never again think the same way about free trade and what it costs.

Seattle, noted Callinicos (1999), turned out to be a 'serious defeat for the official consensus', a consensus where free market capitalism is the dominant *leitmotif*.

2. The Significance of Seattle

What the protestors against globalisation share is dislike of the market economy. (Martin Wolf, *Financial Times*, 8th December 1999)

'Anti-capitalist' is, after all, the term which the protestors themselves use. (Rees, 2000, p.9)

In just over a month, in Seattle, the WTO will hold its 3rd Ministerial Conference—a conference that will launch new trade negotiations, and set the WTO's programme and priorities for the future. This alone would make it an important meeting, but the significance of Seattle goes beyond that. The outcome will be seen as a test of the confidence in the WTO, and a sign of international commitment to trade liberalization. It will influence the direction and credibility of the world trading system as we enter a new and uncertain century. (Michael Moore, Director-General of the WTO, Speech in Berlin, 29th October, in Moore, 1999, p.1)

During the Battle of Seattle and after, many debates occurred regarding its significance.[5] For some socialists, the key point was that Seattle was *against capitalism* (Roberts, 2000). Although there have been many anti-war demonstrations in the past and significant strikes, it could be argued that these forms of struggle targeted the effects and symptoms of the workings of capital. Seattle was against capital *in toto* (as were some other resistances in the series). As Peter Hudis (2000) has argued: Seattle was not just against the WTO, but against what the WTO *stood for*. This was recognised by some right-wing commentators too (as in the Martin Wolf quote above).

On this score, the significance of Seattle was three-fold. First, there was progression from organising on single issues to 'protesting against *capitalism itself*' (Roberts, 2000, p.2). As Wallis argues, capitalism has caused *retrogression* 'in the basic conditions of natural and human existence' (2000, p.152) for millions of people in the last twenty years—including millions in the USA, where real living standards have stagnated or fallen for many. For increasing numbers of people the super-cession of capitalism becomes an urgent, yet more difficult task (as capitalist social relations attain increasing depth and breadth throughout global social existence). Secondly, Tabb (2000b, p.2) noted that 'proposals for confronting transnational capital are in class terms and, for the most part, inclusive'. Seattle and related protests (J18 Carnival Against Capitalism, the demonstrations against the World Economic Forum in Davos and the IMF/World Bank in Washington, and the May Day 2000 events around the world) crystallised class struggles. Thirdly, Seattle, together with other recent anti-capitalist events, has spawned new networks and relationships that can become part of the foundations for further anti-capitalist struggles (Epstein, 2000; Roberts, 2000). Thus, notes Tabb (2000b, p.2): 'A potentially powerful antisystemic movement is at an important point in its development'—with the resources for further anti-capitalist resistance gaining strength. Magnussen and Bernstein (1999) note that Seattle has 'emboldened labor, environmental and other anti-WTO forces to redouble their efforts' (p.34). The significance of organised labour working together with social movements, environmental activists and other radical groups on a scale previously unknown invokes an anti-capitalism of real social substance and significant scale (Brokmeyer, 2000). Roberts points towards the importance of the re-emergence of anti-capitalist solutions that 'signifies a break from the consciousness of the 1990s' (2000, p.2). He notes that the new confidence flowing from Seattle has created the basis for a 'revival of socialist consciousness', especially amongst the youth (*ibid.*).

Yet others were quick to question the significance of Seattle. Magnussen and Bernstein pose the general question:

> [A] week after the tear gas has cleared, the questions linger. Did the scene in Seattle reflect a global *fin de millennium* angst over a world

speeding into uncharted economic and political space? Or is it an
anomaly—a brief conflagration that won't spread? The answers, of
course, won't be known for years to come. (1999, p.4)

Some believed they had the answer straight off. Jenny Bristow (2000),
writing in *LM*, argued that although 'Seattle was self-consciously a protest
'against capitalism' ... [and] ... A protest 'against capitalism' sounds very
bold', this in itself signalled nothing. Rather, argued Bristow, what was really
significant was that at the turn of the century anti-capitalists 'wanted to go
beyond the best that the market could offer, to build on the advances of
capitalism and raise productivity further' (*ibid.*). Whereas today's anti-
capitalists, she argued, timidly call for the reigning in of the productiveness of
capitalism and the tethering of economic growth. Whilst Bristow blithely
ignores the dangers of building socialism upon capitalism's past—specifically
its means of production—and skates over the point that capital is a *social
relation* that requires abolition (Postone, 1996), she opens up the debate to
questioning the real significance of Seattle.[6]

This debate centres on the multi-faceted aims of the Seattle protestors and
elides the revolutionary/reformist distinction. Once we enter this wider debate
the parameters become muddied. One of the strands of the debate was the
notion of democracy. Whilst some, such as Brokmeyer (2000), argued that the
Seattle demonstrations uncovered the 'totally undemocratic essence of
capitalism' (p.2), others (such as Epstein, 2000, p.9) were more concerned
with the narrower issue of the undemocratic nature of the WTO itself. Tabb
(2000b, p.9-10) drew the two issues together: the call for greater democracy
within the WTO expressed a wider demand 'that capital not dominate societal
decision-making' (p.10). Thus:

> ... the demonstrators want to democratize what has been an elite
> decision-making process; to challenge the global dominance of capital
> and capital's state institutions. (Tabb, 2000b, p.1)

The UK Department of Industry and Trade (DTI) spoke with a forked tongue
on this issue. As Bryan Wilson (Minister for Trade) explained, there was a
need to make the WTO more open and democratic and 'To get it right, we will
need to know the views of the British public. This is an exercise in open
government' (DTI, 1999c, p.1). However, Wilson goes on to say that 'we are
already in touch with key representative groups and *opinion formers*, and will
continue to be so. But we are open to *comments from anyone*' (DTI, 1999c,
p.1-2—my emphases). As Caroline Benn and Clyde Chitty (1999) and Richard
Hatcher and Nico Hirtt (1999) indicate, the essential 'opinion formers' for

New Labour are those promoting business interests. Thus, comments from such 'opinion formers' on the future organisation and role of the WTO are not just 'comments from anyone'. They are comments from people who *really* count for New Labour.

A second strand of the debate around the significance of Seattle centred on the extent to which it challenged a particular form of economic growth—the neoliberal model of economic growth. In this model, 'everything must be sacrificed to the free market and to the welfare of business' (Gleeson and Low, 1999/2000, p.19). As the *Economist* put it, the WTO was essential for policing neoliberal economic growth in the sphere of trade policies, relations and practices; without it, it was argued, trade wars would ensue (Economist, 1999c). Thus, to the extent that Seattle challenged neoliberal economic growth, mainstream politicians raised the spectre of chaos in world trade and further deterioration in the lot of the world's poor if the WTO was abolished. For example, the UK Secretary of State for International Development, Clare Short, argued that:

> Those who want to destroy the WTO, the IMF, the World Bank and the rules-based international system would not help the people on whose behalf they claim to speak. Far from producing a more accountable international system, they would create a world where the rich and powerful make the rules between themselves at the expense of the poorest. (Short, 2000)

Short argued that free trade was not the problem (1999c); *poverty* was the issue. She opined that the WTO, International Monetary Fund (IMF) and the World Bank (with the United Nations Conference on Trade and Development (UNCTAD), the International Trade Centre (ITC) and governments of developing countries) could 'ensure that developing countries can use the WTO to advance their interests more effectively' (1999c, p.5). At this point, Short's views meld sweetly with Michael Moore's (WTO Director-General) message that:

> ... the WTO is fundamentally about international solidarity, interdependence, breaking down barriers between people as well as economies. Prosperity and peace—that to me is what the multilateral trading system can bring about. (WTO, 1999a, p.1)

This way forward applied even to areas such as child labour argued Short (1999d).[7] From the Left, those arguing that neoliberalism is the main problem have to convince that this particular response by business and its aids in governments (and in organisations such as the WTO) is not a strategy pursued in order to address deeper economic problems. Thus, they need to convince that neoliberalism is the cause of gross inequalities in standards of living between and within nations, and not a *consequence* of a drive amongst advanced capitalist countries to boost profit rates and gain advantage in trading relations. This shall not be pursued here, but it does raise the deeper issue of whether— in demolishing neoliberalism (as ideology, policy and practice)—capitalism can be 'controlled', for the good of the world's poor and exploited. One alternative is the reconstitution of neo-Keynesian national economic and social reforms as recommended by Chossudovsky (2000). Peter Hudis (2000) and Nick Beams (2000), on the other hand, have argued strongly against any return to the past on the basis that we can 'control' capitalism through regulation. As we argued in *Rethinking Education and Democracy* (Hillcole Group, 1997), radical economic, education and social policies should be advanced that are integral to the establishment of a more equal and just form of society: socialism. Our aims should not be primarily to generate alternative policy ideas for shoring up a defunct capitalism but to argue that these must be linked to *challenging* the nature of contemporary society (Hillcole Group, 1997, p.2).

A third aspect of the post-Seattle debate was that many commentators argued that *globalisation* was the main target at Seattle rather than capitalism *per se* (e.g. Elliott, 2000, p.11; Schwartz, 2000, p.97).[8] Global capitalism could be tamed, or controlled. The key point, therefore, was the role that the WTO could play in the domestication of globalisation. The Left debate on this issue polarises significantly. On the one hand, Colin Hines (2000) has indicated that although 'globalisation cannot be tinkered with', it can be tamed. He advocates *localisation* of trade and productive capacity. However, he does not advocate the transformation of capitalism *per se*—i.e. addressing the very social forces that created globalisation in the first place. On the other hand, there are Left theorists and activists who argue against the notion that globalisation can be detached from capitalism and 'put in its place' (e.g. Beams, 2000; Hudis, 2000). As Thomas indicates: 'Capitalist globalisation *is* capital writ large, capital raging across the world' (2000, p.8—my emphasis).

Fourthly, some (e.g. Epstein, 2000) placed global *corporations* at the centre of the critique of society emanating from Seattle. Furthermore, noted Epstein, there were differences among the various constituencies in Seattle 'over how far the critique of the corporations should go, and what solutions should be proposed to growing corporate power' (2000, p.8). Epstein also read Seattle as a revolt against the general commodification of social life and a yearning for a return to 'community' (especially amongst young people) (2000, p.10).[9] Epstein noted that:

The differences in Seattle over what should be done with the WTO and global corporations were friendly and fluid. Many of the people whom I talked with, from labor, mainstream environmental movements, and the direct action movement, agreed that no one has the answer to the question of how the global economy should be organized, and discussion of these issues must continue. (Epstein, 2000, p.9)

Thus, although differences amongst Seattleites were expressed in a friendly manner, they were real enough and deep enough for Brokmeyer to caution that, by itself, 'the collapse of ... negotiations [in Seattle] cannot be declared a victory for the movement' (2000, p.4).

Some on the Left warned that Seattle would be wasted if protestors continued to prop up old industries with the mantra of 'labor standards' (Amsden, 2000, p.15-16). Many on the Left saw Seattle as embodying new methods of resistance (e.g. alternative media, the Internet, the giant puppets and so on), but for Schwartz (2000) all this missed the point, which was that:

... the WTO is hurtling along at *commercial* pace, while labor is concerned with *generational* and *community* pace (p.96). [Thus, Seattle] ... was a speed bump in the inevitable process of globalization. The juggernaut has hardly been slowed, and the pace of commercial culture will race on at Internet speed (p.97).

Whilst the point here is not to summarise all the views regarding the significance of Seattle, a range of perspectives has been hinted at. Certainly, if nothing else, Seattle has generated a new wave of debates and discussions on a vast range of issues, socialist strategy and on 'what is to be done' next by the Left. Tabb (2000b) argues that these are hard times for the Left, and the significance of Seattle is whether it can be viewed retrospectively as a real turning point for labour in the struggle against capital. He notes, however, that it is difficult to discern turning points, but 'Seattle may prove just such an event' (p.17).

After Seattle

What is to be done after Seattle is a question many people including (but not only) activists, now confront. (William Tabb, 2000b, p.2)

The anti-capitalist movement may not succeed to incite global change but with Japan hosting the G8 summit early this July and the IMF holding an Autumn meeting in September, anarchist websites are once more alive with messages inciting browsers to protest. (Haynes, 2000, p.37).

As well as discussion on the significance of Seattle, there has been considerable debate regarding what the anti-capitalist movement does next. Tabb (2000b) has called for a deepening of the critique of the WTO, whilst setting out the limitations of reformist demands advanced by what he calls 'mainstream' critics of the WTO. Tabb summarises his approach as:

> ... an analysis of both the corporate media's response to the demonstrations in Seattle and the real issues of class power relations. It is an analysis which focuses on corporate control of policy making, addressing policies which weaken unions and diminish the lives and agency of working people, reduce the sphere of public service provision, and pit one community of workers against another. To this basic class analysis, environmentalists have added a powerful critique of corporate greed and of the single-minded pursuit of accumulation, which threatens the planet and all living things. (2000b, p.2)

However, argues Tabb, as well as analysis, the anti-capitalist movement requires a 'radical vision', as:

> Change does not come about from the mere fact of oppression. In the absence of hope for meaningful change, a sense that a better alternative exists and is possible, pessimism and cynicism prevail. A radical vision consists first of anger at the way things are, the feeling that conditions are intolerable, but if this is to lead beyond thoughtless and futile rebellion, it must be accompanied by a belief that a better alternative is not only desirable but possible; not necessarily tomorrow, but when the momentum can be turned around. Resistance can have a strong element of moral witness (speaking truth to power), of rebellion (I'm mad and I won't take it anymore), of reformist goals (our mutual ideas are violated, let us live up to our agreed upon principles), and of revolutionary transformation (the institutions of structured inequality and destruction are necessary to preserve their power, the system must be overthrown, and a fundamentally different one put in its place). Each of these stances was visible at Seattle. (2000b, p.15)

In the last few years, other socialists have argued that a 'socialist vision' is necessary (e.g. Paula Allman, 1999), whilst yet others (such as Moishe Postone, 1996) have pinpointed the gap between how things are (in capitalism) and possibilities for human life after the abolition of capital. Given the 'once bitten twice shy' complex following the collapse of the terrible old Eastern Bloc states, others have argued that some sort of minimal redprint is necessary now, whereas for Marx it was not such a big issue (Shepherd, 1993). Today, people need some reassurance that they are not helping to set in train a process that ultimately engulfs them in a new maelstrom of oppression. Neumann urges that we need an anti-capitalist movement that does 'not recreate the violence we are protesting against' yet nevertheless holds a 'place for rage' (2000, p.92).[10] Elliott argues that the post-Seattle scene requires 'a mission statement, a credo, that gives the movement, such as it is, some focus' (1999, p.29).

What to do with the WTO is a key topic: reform or abolition being the main divide (Lacayo, 1999), but generally how to lessen the secrecy shrouding the WTO's decision-making processes. Lowe argues that national governments will not challenge either the WTO's secrecy or its dictats—therefore we must defend ourselves (2000, p.68).

For Naomi Klein (in Lowe, 2000), any 'alternative' (such as Seattle) is quickly incorporated within the capitalist marketing machine—*a la* Che Guevara T-shirts and TV adverts featuring Lenin dubbed to speak pro-capitalist inanities—therefore, the task is to take on consumer capitalism. As Klein notes, Seattle shows that:

> In a world in which all that is 'alternative' is sold as soon as it appears, where any innovation or subversion is immediately adopted by un-radical, faceless corporations, gradually, tentatively, a new— our—generation is beginning to fight consumerism with its own best weapons. (Naomi Klein, from her book *No Logo*, in Lowe, 2000, p.68).

Callinicos (1999) posits Seattle as spawning many different conceptions of societies alternative to capitalism. After Seattle and other recent anti-capitalist events, argues Callinicos, a range of conceptions of societies alternative to capitalism are emerging, and:

> In the coming years these alternatives will be tested, in debate and in struggle, till the movements they inspire bring the great edifice of capitalism tumbling down. (1999, p.4)

Questions regarding 'what to do next' are central to the struggle. This pamphlet goes on to make suggestions regarding a *few* of the things worth a try. Specifically, it raises the issue of education as an area where anti-capitalist strategies can hit the edifice of global capitalism, hard.

3. Seattle, the WTO and Education

Education policy is not distinct from a local response to globalisation, it is part of globalisation. In other words, globalisation has an integral education dimension. It is not being devised primarily at the level of each separate nation-state. The increasingly transnational nature of capital means that capital develops its education agenda on a transnational basis. (Hatcher and Hirtt, 1999, p.21)

Yes, globalization is going to be all over everything—education, health, communication, capital, knowledge. (Jacques Rogozinski, Deputy General Manager of Inter-American Corp., in Elliott, 1999/ 2000, p.65)

On the surface, Seattle did not appear to have much to do with education. From press and Internet accounts, education did not seem to rate as highly as many other issues. The environment, the power of transnational corporations, the undemocratic nature of the WTO, the WTO's in-built bias against the interests of Third World nations, globalisation, trade liberalisation, the plight of small farmers and businesses and many other issues—all seemed to be far more significant. Education figured as a spin-off issue in relation to the more prominent issue of child labour. Some critics of the WTO's attitude to child labour (e.g. AFL-CIO, 1999) and some of those who believed a reformed WTO could make an impact on the need for child labour (e.g. Short, 1999a-b) tended to view the abolition of child labour as precursor to education for the poor.[11] Yet, as this section shows, education was a key issue for Seattle. It's strategic importance increased post-Seattle.

This was perceived immediately in the 'Seattle spins' energised by WTO apologists. Prior to Seattle, many mainstream journalists and commentators talked about the 'ignorance' of the anti-WTO protestors gathering in Seattle. They were presented as 'Senseless in Seattle' or 'Rebels without a Clue' (Gleeson and Low, 1999/2000, p.19). This abuse extended also to the anti-World Economic Forum (WEF) protestors at Davos. Pontin, for instance, labelled the Davos protestors as 'sentimental, arrogant and ignorant' (2000, p.488). The protestors were called 'militant dunces [who] parade their ignorance through the streets of Seattle' (Economist, 1999c), or as being simply 'confused' (Stephens, 1999, p.19). Mike Moore, Director-General of the WTO, in his Opening Address to the 3rd Ministerial Conference in Seattle, labelled the protestors neither 'bad nor mad'; but they were misinformed and were 'wrong to blame the WTO for all the world's problems' (WTO, 1999b, p.2). Stephen

Byers (UK Secretary of State, Department of Trade and Industry), in his speech at Seattle, argued that there was a big job to do to convince people that globalisation and trade liberalisation 'can be a decisive force for good' (Byers, 1999b, p.2). He argued that to win the 'intellectual debate' was crucial (*ibid.*).

For others (e.g. Klee, 1999; Economist, 1999c), it was clear that the Seattle protestors were all-too-well educated on the issues. Klee pointed towards how the 'Naderites and other groups posted Web pages to educate their followers on the evils of foreign trade' (1999, p.23) and the importance of going to Seattle. The *Economist* lamented the fact that: 'Long before the WTO summit started on November 30th, 2, 500 campaigners attended a packed teach-in on the evils of globalisation' (Economist, 1999b, p.55).

Post-Seattle, the need for a wider educational offensive by pro-WTOers was recognised. Smith and Moran note that:

> In the United States, trade officials now talk of 'educating constituents' on the benefits of free trade. Within a week of the Seattle meetings the WTO completely overhauled its Web site, incorporating a new 'global town hall' and Letterman-like 'Top 10 Lists' extolling the 'benefits' and de-fogging the 'common misunderstandings' of the WTO. (2000, p.66)

Smith and Moran also pointed out the educational challenge facing the Left post-Seattle:

> Our job on the left is to project a critique of WTO-style trade liberalization and economic liberalization more broadly. We need to incorporate these issues into research agendas, classroom curricula, and popular discourse. Efforts to construct a world based on social justice and ecological sustainability depend on democratic participation. Cultivating the public awareness and civic skills for such democratic participation is a fundamental challenge for the left at the beginning of the twenty-first century. (2000, p. 70)

It seems then that the meaning of 'Seattle' will remain an educational battleground for some time to come. For the Left, it is likely to remain an educational resource for time immemorial (with an impressive range of video, Internet and print material available).

The 3rd Ministerial Conference at Seattle had direct relevance for education. One of the key aims of the meeting was to expand significantly the role and reach of the WTO into areas such as financial services, health care and *education* (Smith and Moran, 2000, p.66). Seattle was not just about narrow conceptions of 'trade' or the 'economy', notes De Angelis (2000, p.10); the

WTO was furthering its aims throughout all spheres of society. It was set to construct a wider mandate in Seattle (Reese, 1999, p.4). Thus:

> Every commodity and service was to be declared open to free trade—from turnips to school textbooks, from intellectual ideas to health provision. Any state subsidy in any of these areas could be declared a barrier to free trade. (Rees, 2000, p.9)

The Seattle protests, therefore, delayed substantial gearing up in the liberalisation and privatisation of education and other services. Prior to Seattle, Charlene Barshefsky (U.S. Trade Representative) had been calling for a more comprehensive incorporation of health care and education into the WTO's orbits (Working Group on the WTO/MAI, 1999, p.14). As Abbie Bakan noted:

> One of the most profound changes in the politics of world trade is the formal definition of services as a trade barrier. The increasing privatisation of healthcare services in Canada and Britain has already provided a taste of things to come if supporters of free market policies have their way. The WTO agenda includes proposals to challenge state support for services which inhibit the flow of international capital. ... Education is also on the list. (2000a, p.24)

As George Monbiot (2000, p.15) pointed out, the measures to have been discussed in Seattle (had not the protestors been so successful in disrupting proceedings) would have forced governments 'to privatise their key public services, including welfare, housing, health and *education*' (my emphasis). GATS terms require every WTO member government to deregulate every service sector—and Seattle would have speeded this process up (Working Group on the WTO/MAI, 1999). The WTO agenda is aimed at the eventual abolition of all local systems for regulating trade in any good or service in order to create a so-called global 'level playing field' (Balanya *et al*, 1999/2000, p.11). Nico Hirtt has pointed out that as early as 1995 the WTO concluded the first general agreement on the liberalisation of services (GATS), and education 'featured there explicitly' (2000, p.14). Only education systems financed absolutely by the state and with total exclusion of any commercial operations were excluded. As Hirtt concluded: 'There are few education systems which correspond to this profile' (*ibid.*).

Price, Pollock and Shaoul report there has been scant public recognition regarding how 'the privatisation of public services at national level is linked to the global trade-expansion policies of international institutions, such as the WTO, the International Monetary Fund, and the World Bank' (1999, p.1889). The WTO GATS agreements cover 160 service sectors, from telecoms to leisure services. As Hirtt notes, it is 'not necessary to see the word 'education' figuring on the agenda of a negotiation for education to be effectively involved in it' (2000, p.14). It is included in the catchall term 'services' along with the other 159 sectors. GATS are founded upon 'an agenda aimed at progressively liberalising services' (*ibid.*). However, and in part because of WTO Council for Trade in Services (CTS) subterfuge over wording:

> What few people realise is that health care, social services, education, housing, and other services run by government agencies are also included. (Price, Pollock and Shaoul, 1999, p.1889)

Price, Pollock and Shaoul argue that as profitability in manufacturing has declined, U.S. and EU corporations have 'turned to services as an alternative source of profit' (*ibid.*). On official U.S. data, cross-border sales of education services by U.S companies to foreign purchasers totalled $8.3 billion in 1997 (WTO/CTS, 1998b, p.1). Bakan (2000a, p.24) notes that:

> According to a document obtained by the Canadian Association of University Teachers (CAUT), US companies specialising in the export of private educational services—such as branch campuses, 'virtual education', and the international marketing of curricula and academic programs—gleaned US$7 billion in 1996 alone. This is the fifth largest service sector in the US. 'Barriers' to further market expansion are now to be eliminated, according to the WTO, and such barriers include educational practices that inhibit 'innovation', and any form of subsidies for students, including bus passes.

Education is big business. The main WTO weapon for opening educational services up to corporate capital is procurement agreements—whereby public sector services have to provide a 'level playing' field for all the goods and services they buy in. This 'opens up domestic services and markets to international competition' (Price, Pollock and Shaoul, 1999, p.1891). Price, Pollock and Shaoul were in no doubt about the significance of Seattle for the public services:

> The WTO is stage-managing a new privatisation bonanza at Seattle. Multinational and transnational corporations, including the pharmaceutical, insurance, and service sectors, are lining up to capture the chunks of gross domestic product that governments currently spend on public services such as education and health. The long tradition of European welfare states based on solidarity through community risk-pooling and publicly accountable services is being dismantled. (p.1892)

They argued that domestic opposition to privatisation could hold this process in check. However, for education in the UK and in and in other EU countries,[12] the 'neo-liberal agenda for education is now sweeping with gathering speed through the school and college systems of Europe and the other advanced capitalist countries', according to Hatcher and Hirtt (1999, p.22). In the UK context, recent announcements by Education Secretary David Blunkett on the future of comprehensive education confirm Hatcher and Hirtt's analysis of what is going on. According to Bright (2000a), latest changes to compulsory schooling in the UK 'will effectively consign the comprehensive system—the great egalitarian dream of the Sixties—to history'. Bright points towards the prospect of increased specialisation within compulsory schooling, with children taking lessons in a range of institutions, in some cases 'from teachers in the private sector' (*ibid.*). According to Bright: 'Boots the Chemist and Reg Vardy, the north-east car dealer, are already involved in plans to set up new schools'.[13] This is all of a piece with the strategy of the UK's Department of Trade and Industry (DTI). That is to break down any 'remaining trade barriers' and to work for the 'deepening and broadening [of] liberalisation of trade in services and establish a liberal, rules-based framework for international investment' (Byers, 1999a, p.10).

In 1998, the WTO stepped up its work on education. Its Council for Trade in Services (CTS) published two reports (WTO/CTS, 1998a, b) that set out perspectives on education and trade in educational services. The first report of the WTO/CTS argued for the significance of education in generating economic growth and also for reductions in social inequalities. It argued that education enabled individuals and nations to be integrated into processes of economic and social development and enabled them to be fully prepared for integration into global commercial networks (p.2). The key point, it was argued, was that education provides the skills for effective participation (for individuals and countries) in all these respects. It promotes the development of human capital.

What this first report made clear was that *basic* education (i.e. elementary, compulsory and basic skills education for adults) provided by the state 'may be considered to fall within the domain of, in the terminology of the GATS' (WTO/CTS, 1998a, p.4). The report recognised, however, that the private sector had a relatively small role to play in these fields in many countries as compared with the input from the state. The key areas yielding substantial private sector investment were in distance learning, computer-based learning systems, educational media products (in cable and satellite transmission) and audio and video conferencing. PC software, CD-ROMs and the Internet were three other significant fields of educational development involving the private sector. The main category of trade in educational services concerned students taking up education outside their country of domicile—and here the WTO/CTS questioned the need for immigration and currency controls that were effective barriers to student mobility (1998a, p.8). Finally, the report raised the issue of education-related services that were 'not instructional in nature'—such as college selection services, educational consultants, counselling services, student exchange programmes and educational testing services—on where they stood in terms of agreements on 'education'. The report praised the efforts of EU countries to deregulate education, especially higher education. Top marks went to the UK government, which since the 1980s, has undertaken 'a movement away from public financing, and towards greater market responsiveness, coupled with an increasing openness to alternative financing mechanisms'[14] (in Hirtt, 2000, p.14).

The second WTO/CTS report (1998b) hailed the benefits of liberalisation of trade in educational services. The main arguments advanced were that it increased diversity and choice of educational services for WTO members. For 'emerging economies', in need of 'technology-savvy' and 'well-trained' workforces that are able to compete in the global economy' liberalisation of trade in educational services was deemed 'vital' (WTO/CTS, 1998b, p.1). It was argued that growth in educational services, 'including the sale of education of education and training, materials and equipment' would raise demand for related services and goods (*ibid.*). The Secretariat to the WTO/CTS went on to note that:

> ... WTO members have made fewer commitments for education services than any other service area except for energy services. However, this is balanced by the fact that a number of countries have made substantial commitments in higher education-plus categories, so the basis exists for broader liberalization. (WTO/CTS, 1998b, p.2)

Clearly, the education sector was being singled out for special treatment as an area where openness to private corporations was at far less than the desired level. WTO members were admonished for their under-performance in liberalising trade in education services. Thus:

> It would be useful for WTO members to establish a common understanding that such openness to foreign service providers leads to economic growth and for the WTO members who have not yet made commitments in this sector to give serious thought to doing so. (WTO/ CTS, 1998b, p.2)

To realise this objective, in 1999 (at the behest of the CTS) and looking forward to the Seattle Ministerial Conference, the WTO Secretariat set up a working group that was to explore possibilities for increased liberalisation of educational services. (Hirtt, 2000, p.14).

As Mike Moore, Director-General of the WTO, promised: 'Despite the temporary setback in Seattle, our objectives remain unchanged' (WTO, 1999c, p.2)—which includes the WTO agenda for the liberalisation of trade in educational services and the privatisation of education. Nico Hirtt warns us that, post-Seattle, education 'will still be a question for the WTO in the coming three years' (2000, p.14). As Stephens (1999, p.19) notes: 'The new Europe is being made by corporations not politicians'.

Interestingly, the newest WTO member—China—has recently signed 'a wide-ranging framework education agreement' with the UK (DfEE, 2000, p.1). This framework agreement 'will give new impetus to bilateral relations in education and training between the United Kingdom and China' (*ibid.*). The UK Department for Education and Employment (DfEE) announced the agreement as:

> ... a significant step in building partnerships between two important players in the global economy. Information and Communication Technology is a key asset in helping people and business adapt to and harness the opportunities of the world economy' (*ibid.*).

The DfEE document went on to eulogise that:

> Both countries realise the importance of the knowledge-based economy to our success and prosperity. Lifelong learning is now a key strategy in equipping people with the skills they need; in developing a learning society in which everyone, from whatever background, routinely expects to learn and upgrade their skills throughout life. ... Sharing our expertise and experiences in the fields of basic education, lifelong learning, and vocational and higher education will be of mutual benefit in equipping our people to contribute to, and enjoy the benefits and opportunities of, the global economy. (*ibid.*)

Perhaps this will prove to be a not-so-gentle first step for China as an introduction to WTO membership and the underpinning urge to integrate into the global capitalist economy. At least it might get China and the UK some gold stars from the WTO/CTS.

4. The Significance of Education for Anti-Capitalism[15]

This section moves from the opposite direction: what is the significance of education for post-Seattle anti-capitalist strategies? In answering this question, a deeper question is posed: why does education appear to be so significant in contemporary capitalist society? What was the social substance (rather than the electioneering) behind Tony Blair's pre-1997 election mantra: 'education, education, education'?

Providing answers to these deeper questions requires going back to a great nineteenth-century thinker: Karl Marx. It is well known that Karl Marx begins his first volume of *Capital* with the commodity, not capital. Marx first of all draws our attention to the fact that:

> The wealth of those societies in which the capitalist mode of production prevails, presents itself as 'an immense accumulation of commodities', its unit being a single commodity. Our investigation must therefore begin with the analysis of a commodity. (Marx, 1867a, p.43)[16]

For Marx, the analysis of capitalism begins with the commodity as it is the 'economic cell-form' (Marx, 1867b, p.19) of that society. It is the most simple and basic element that can inform us about more complex phenomena springing from it, in the same way that human DNA provides significant data on the more concrete features of humans in general and particular individuals. Moreover, value is not something that can be directly observed; thus:

> In the analysis of economic forms ... neither microscopes nor chemical reagents are of use. The force of abstraction must replace both. ... [And to] ... the superficial observer, the analysis of these forms seems to turn upon minutiae. It does in fact deal with minutiae, but they are of the same order as those dealt with in microscopic anatomy. (*ibid.*)

The commodity was the perfect starting point for Marx as it incorporates the basic structuring elements of capitalist society: value, use-value and exchange-value posited on the basis of abstract labour as measured by labour-time (Postone, 1996, p.127-128). It is the condensed 'general form of the product' in capitalist society (*ibid.*, 148), the 'most elementary form of bourgeois wealth' (Marx, 1863, p.173), and hence the 'formation and premise of capitalist production' (Marx, 1866, p.1004). Commodities are also 'the first result of the immediate process of capitalist production, its product' (Marx, 1866, p.974).

In *Theories of Surplus Value—Part One* (Marx, 1863), Marx makes it clear that there are two classes or categories of commodities within the social universe of capital, as:

> The whole world of 'commodities' can be divided into two great parts. First, labour-power; second, commodities as distinct from labour-power itself. (Marx, 1863, p.167)

Labour-power is the capacity to labour; a potential to labour that has a virtual form of existence at the level of the labour market. However, Marx notes that within the labour process itself, labour-power attains *real* social existence. As it is transformed into labour on the activation of relevant powers, capacities and skills etc. for labouring in a particular labour process, it becomes a real social force (Rikowski, 2000c). This is implied in Marx's definition of labour-power as:

> ... the aggregate of those mental and physical capabilities existing in a human being, which he exercises whenever he produces a use-value of any description. (1867a, p.164)

Thus, when we are engaged in producing material or immaterial commodities in the labour process, which take the concrete form of use-values (useful products), our labour-powers attain social reality. The activation of the attributes of labour-power (the pertinent skills, attitudes etc.) is ultimately dependent upon the *will* of the labourer. This will-determined aspect is built into Marx's definition of labour-power above—'which he exercises'—and this is a fact that representatives of capital (as managers, human resource experts and so on) never cease to worry about: the 'motivation problem' endlessly discussed in management journals.

The two classes of commodities are distinguished essentially on the following consideration:

> A *commodity*—as distinguished from labour-power itself—is a material thing confronting man, a thing of a certain utility for him, in which a definite quantity of labour is fixed or materialised. (Marx, 1863, p.164—original emphasis)[17]

Later on in *Theories of Surplus Value, Part One* Marx criticises Adam Smith for holding that the commodity, in order to incorporate value, has to be a physical, *material* thing. Value is a *social* substance; it has therefore a social mode of existence. Thus:

> When we speak of the commodity as a materialisation of labour—
> in the sense of its exchange-value—this is only an imaginary, that is to
> say, a purely *social mode* of existence of the commodity *which has*
> *nothing to do with its corporeal reality*; it is conceived as a definite
> quantity of social labour or of money. (Marx, 1863, p.171—my
> emphases).

Unfortunately, Marx confuses the issue by referring to 'material
commodities' and commodities as 'objects' elsewhere. It should not be forgotten
that Marx wrote *Capital* for the workers (whilst also trying to impress German
professors). The examples he uses in *Capital* to illustrate his arguments relating
to commodities were nearly all of the material, 'object' kind: coats, linen, iron
paper and so on. In the first volume of *Capital*, Marx states that: 'A commodity
is, in the first place, an object outside us, a *thing* that by its properties satisfies
human wants of some sort or another' (1867a, p.43—my emphasis). Here, he
seems to be ruling out products such as transport, drama performances and
education (examples that he had ruled *in* as commodities in *Theories of Surplus*
Value: Part One) as instances of commodities. He rules out *immaterial*
commodities. Without going deeper into the issue here, I would maintain that
a really radical and significant interpretation of Marx would start out from the
commodity as inclusive of material and immaterial forms (and Lazzarato, 1996
contains an interesting discussion on this issue). Indeed, the distinction between
material and immaterial commodities is practically dissolving on a daily basis.
The commodity form (commodification) is taking hold of all spheres of social
existence.

This last point is crucial. Marx's original distinction between labour-power
and the 'general class' of commodities was that the latter were *external* to the
person of the labourer, whereas labour-power was incorporated within
personhood itself. However, with people buying cosmetic surgery, the market
in spare body parts and the future beckoning big business in human design
and re-design facilities (Joy, 2000), the physical externality of the 'general
class' of commodities to human beings is no longer what it was in Marx's day.
These developments herald the breakdown of this aspect of Marx's original
distinction between the two great classes of commodities. What, then, is the
distinction between the two categories of commodities if the externality
criterion is no longer what it was?

It could be argued that a distinction still exists between the two great classes
on the following considerations. First, labour-power is an aspect of the person;
it is *internal* to personhood, in a special sense. It is a unified *force* flowing
throughout the person. The installation of a new heart—an object originally

Glenn Rikowski

external to the person in question, or an artificial hip joint—does not chaɪ.ᵍͼ this. Labour-power has no *specific* location within personhood; it is a force flowing throughout the totality of the person. Labour-power has reality *only* within the person, whereas general commodities have existence external to the person *and* can also become elements of persons, as increasing numbers of medical products become incorporated within the human. Labour-power, as a human force, cannot leave humans and, for example, act as the same force within bricks. As Marx noted, labour power does 'not exist apart from him [the labourer] at all' (Marx, 1858, p.267). It cannot be *external* to the person (though items of the 'general class' of commodities can be part of personhood). Marx notes the 'uniqueness' of labour power in this respect (1863, p.45). Secondly, labour power (unlike a brick) is under the sway of a potentially hostile will. Internality and consciousness distinguish labour power from the general class of commodities.

However, it could be argued that some animals have a capacity to labour (e.g. pit ponies, dray horses, police dogs), and *also* have consciousness. A final point presents human labour power as qualitatively different from animal labour power: socially average *human* labour power uniquely *constitutes value.* It is *socially average* human labour-power that is the foundation of the *abstract labour* that forms value. Abstract labour rests upon the *socially necessary labour time* required to produce any use value under conditions normal for a given society, and this *presupposes* socially average human labour power (Marx, 1867a; Neary and Rikowski, 2000, p.20-21). Human labour-power at the *socially average* constitutes value, not concrete (directly observable) labour (Marx, 1867a). No other commodity (either living or dead) has this unique capacity. Wo(men) are the 'measure of all things'; the social universe of capital is constituted, and its most fundamental social forms (value and capital) are created and mediated (in their transformations), by us. Yet capital, as social force and relation, comes to dominate us, its progenitors (Postone, 1996).

Labour-power, on this account, is the special commodity that generates value (the substance of capital), and hence capital itself. Without human labour-power, there is no capital—no matter what the level of technological development (Rikowski, 2000b). The capitalist labour process, and the labour performed within it, incorporates a duality: the production of commodities that have use-value (they are useful products) and also incorporate *value.* Value is the social *substance* of capital, indeed of the whole social universe of capital (Neary and Rikowski, 2000).

The centrality of labour-power to the maintenance and expansion of the social universe of capital fixes the significance of education and training in contemporary capitalist society. These are intimately involved in the *social production of labour-power*; that unique, living commodity that has the capacity to generate more value (*surplus* value) than is required to maintain its social existence *as* labour-power. Marx's theory of surplus value (in Marx, 1867a) rests on this point. Education and training in capitalism, on this analysis, have a key role in socially producing the special commodity (labour-power) that generates value, surplus value and *capital itself*, as the first form that capital appears is as surplus value. Surplus value is the lifeblood of capital, or the social energy that brings capital (and *profit* as an offshoot of capital) to life.

In capitalist society, labour-power takes the form of 'human capital', the human *as capital*. Labour-power is inseparable from the labourer and includes not just 'skills', capacities and competencies but also incorporates the work attitudes and personality traits for effective performance in the labour process (Rikowski, 2000c). Thus, labour-power is an aspect of personhood itself. Insofar as education and training are processes for labour-power production then they are also involved in the *capitalisation of humanity*.

The social drive to enhance the quality of labour-power derives from the fact that, everything else being equal, capitalist enterprises with higher quality labour-powers will create more value and surplus value: workers labour harder, faster, more effectively. As Mike Cole (1998, 1999) and myself (2000a-b) have indicated, this process is ratcheted up with the intensification of globalisation in the last ten years. New Labour's education policy has human capital development as one of its key guiding threads (Cole, 1999). New Labour seeks to make UK capital competitive through this strategy, argues Cole (1998), hoping to attract inward investment and establish the UK as a leading 'knowledge economy' (Rikowski, 2000a). The project of 'modernisation' of schools and other sectors in education is linked to these national goals (Cole, 1998, 1999). Teachers are central actors in New Labour's business agenda for schools based on 'modernisation' for national economic gaols (Allen, 1999).[18] Education for the nation!

After Marx

Prime Minister Tony Blair, Secretary of State for Education and Employment David Blunkett and other Ministers have sought to justify their stress on human capital development as being necessary for competitiveness on the global economic stage. On their message, there must be continual updating and re-definition of labour-power attributes (skills, attitudes etc.) in order to ensure that the nation's human capital is up to the mark. This is necessary for economic survival but also for social cohesion, these Ministers, their acolytes and their academic protagonists argue. The turmoil caused by having to change jobs more frequently (increasingly to short-term contracts) creates a task for the state to legitimate the whole process as the working class is continually recomposed. As Massimo de Angelis (2000, p.10) argues:

> Education is crucial for capital if it wants to rely on a strategy of continuous displacement of the class composition. An educated worker in today's paradigm is a worker who is able to adapt—who is able to take one job one day and another job the next day—who is engaged in life-long learning as a continuous process, which means updating their skills to suit the market. That is essential to maintain social cohesion in a context in which there is continuous displacement of the class composition, of what kind of work is done.

De Angelis notes that a recent document from the International Labour Office talks about 'competitive societies' and their need to hit the right balance between wealth-creation and social cohesion (*ibid.*). De Angelis argues that education has a central role to play in ensuring a sustainable balance between the two.

What is clear is that as the globalisation of capital progresses, nations seek to gain competitive advantage through generating higher levels of labour-power quality. The question of whether they *in fact* succeed in this (the perennial question of much research and writing on post-compulsory education and training) partly misses the point. In contemporary society, we are *driven* to enhance labour-power quality, no matter what the actual results. This flows from the fact that all of capital's social drives are *infinite*; with no resting-place—no end point, where the satisfaction of a drive can be realised (Rikowski, 2000b). In tandem with the Rolling Stones, capital 'can't get no satisfaction'! Concretely, the infinite social drive to enhance labour-power quality expresses itself in a myriad of education policies and outlooks; 'raising standards' (to ever higher levels); school improvement (you can *always* improve); attaining better 'human capital' than this or that competitor (with no *end* to the process possible). 'Can do better' says more on the analysis presented here, and becomes more sinister, than when used by the most malevolent of school report writers! Of course, concrete expressions of an infinite drive cannot be themselves expressed infinitely, unless we assume infinite conditions: time, money, materials, quality of labour-power and so on. These considerations point towards practical and social impossibilities, and, at the extreme, logical absurdities. The silliest consequence is that we have to assume infinite quality of labour-powers in the producers (e.g. teachers) in order to produce it in pupils. The social universe of capital has madness at its heart. Lunacies within education such as those outlined above drive us on in capitalist society; to more stress, teacher suicides, alienation as teachers and students. Worst of all perhaps, we collude in processes of capitalisation of our own souls insofar as we are engaged in aiding the reduction of humanity to labour-power through education and training. *Awareness* of this process, whilst causing uneasiness, is a crucial first step towards successfully challenging this situation—though not sufficient in itself, for a *collective* project for rescuing education from capital is essential, as the demolition of capitalist social relations in their entirety must be pursued (Rikowski, 1999). No amount of 'reflexivity', posing as a 'reflective practitioner', indulging in textual deconstruction or sophistry can evade this.

The WTO's drive to open up education to business compounds and confuses the situation further. Hatcher and Hirtt (1999) point towards an important distinction between the school as the producer of human capital on the one hand, and as a site for profitable enterprise on the other. There is therefore, a possible tension between these two goals. It is logically possible that handing schools over to business interests may run counter to the attempt by national governments to raise UK labour-power quality. The small-scale (but increasingly significant) interventions of the private sector in running schools can be viewed as crucial tests of whether these two goals are compatible.[19] The case of Nord Anglia's involvement at the Islington Arts and Media School is a weather vane (Bright, 2000b).

On the other hand, as Martin Allen has argued at some of our Hillcole meetings, New Labour does not recognise the traditional difference between the public and private sectors. New Labour is concerned with 'what works' (Rikowski, 2000d). Thus, if it can be shown that international corporations running schools can raise 'standards' (however measured) as proxy indicators of human capital quality then tensions between profit-making in education and raising human capital quality may not be prohibitively acute. This convenient result can be made even more likely if the general public can be persuaded (on a progressive scale) to pay for their own development as labour-power (the institution of student fees for higher education being particularly important in this context).

Historically, of course, capitalist enterprises, particularly in Britain, have been loath to invest in developing labour-power. This is so for two main reasons. First, labour-power (incorporated within personhood) cannot be sold in capitalist society (as that would involve a form of direct slavery) within its formally 'free' labour market. Although representatives of capital must buy labour-power, and may make a formal contribution to its social production (e.g. work-based training), they clearly have problems in producing it for sale *per se*.[20] Of course, various forms of fees and transfer payments (e.g. in professional football—a practice currently approaching termination in the

European Union) are attempts to get round this point on the part of capitalist enterprises. The second point, related to the first, is that in a formally 'free' labour market, labourers can sell their labour-powers to whatever capitalist enterprise they strike up a bargain with. Thus, firms spending on labour-power development cannot be sure that workers will not receive training and then take off, with some other enterprise benefiting. In some trades, workers may gain skills within a business and then set up on their own in direct competition to their previous employers (as in the horological industry, see Rikowski, 2000e). These two factors together place *practical* constraints on the *infinite* social drive to increase labour-power quality (though there are others—not discussed here). How societies deal with this situation (in education and training policies for stimulating human capital development) will vary, but the underlying material constraints bite in all capitalist societies.

The Pay-Off

The analysis of this section enables a further answer to the question of the significance of Seattle for education. There are two parts to this answer. First, Seattle challenges both neo-liberalism and globalisation. As Dave Hill (1999) has shown, New Labour's education policy since 1997 is basically *neo-liberal* in its design. Furthermore, as Mike Cole (1999) demonstrates, New Labour's education policy is a specific response to globalisation: its attempt to ensure competitiveness through human capital development. Finally, Cole (1998) and Martin Allen (1999) have pointed towards the 'modernisation' of schools and teachers' work being undertaken by New Labour, to make both more businesslike and more business oriented; the 'businessification' of schooling (Allen, 1999, p.24). Seattle poses an implicit challenge to this entire package; in challenging neo-liberalism and globalisation it undercuts the whole *logic* of New Labour's education policy. New Labour is designing education policy for a future whose realisation is being challenged by anti-capitalists.

The second point flowing from the analysis of this section is more crucial. In section 2, the debate around the significance of Seattle did not include education as a leading reference point. However, the analysis here indicates the significance of education and training for the post-Seattle debate concerning 'what to do next'. It highlights the *strategic importance* of education and training in capitalist society as elements in the social production of labour-power in capitalism. Education and training are implicated in the social production of the *one commodity underpinning the maintenance of capitalist society*: labour-power. This is capitalism's weakest link. Furthermore, in order to move beyond capitalist society, collectively we shall have to devise forms of labour-power expenditure, development (i.e. new forms of education and training) *not tied to the value-form of labour.* These considerations indicate the real social power of teachers and trainers in contemporary society. They are guardians of the development of the one commodity that keeps capitalism going, whilst also being in a structural position to *subvert the smooth flow of labour power production* by inserting principles antagonistic to the social domination of capital. Such principles include social justice, equality and solidarity for progressive social change. Most significantly, teachers are structurally well placed to raise awareness of, and to generate an educational and wider politics for, *human resistance to our capitalisation*; resistance to our humanity being reduced to labour-power (i.e. human capital). Teachers are dangerous to capital and its social domination on these counts—a point both New Labour and Tory administrations instinctively grasp (and which is manifested in attempts to control the curriculum and teachers' work).

On the analysis provided here, activists and others participating in the post-Seattle debate and struggles against global capitalism could do worse than consider capitalist education and training as key sites for the disruption of the everyday workings of capitalist society. Furthermore, education and training are key institutions for social transformation and the post-capitalist society of the future. This is the significance of education and training after Seattle. To advance this insight practically, it is essential to work on *alternatives* to capitalist education and training: to offer a way forward after critique. The Conclusion addresses this issue.

Conclusion: The Question of Alternatives

> ... we must create new organizations and a new political language that can unify international groups into collective protest action. We are challenged to build new political networks and information sharing ... We must make the connections in the fight for democracy in the 21st century. (Manning Marable, *Seattle and Beyond: Making the Connection in the 21st Century*, 2000)

> One of the big battles that we have to face is to constitute a different horizon, a different perspective, of where we are going and where we want to go. (Massimo de Angelis, *Enclosure and Integration*, 2000)

This pamphlet has demonstrated that education—far from being a marginal issue in Seattle—was at the heart of the action. The immediate significance of the Battle in Seattle for education is that it has delayed the WTO agenda for education: liberalisation of trade in educational services and the privatisation of education. The WTO's impatience with member states for making slow progress on this agenda means that the pressure is still on for more. The opening quotation to the previous section (from Hatcher and Hirtt, 1999, p.21) suggests that education policies increasingly shadow developments within global capital. The imperative is on the WTO to lay the foundations for reconfiguring global labour-power through education and training policies conducive to transnational corporations.

As Martin Allen (1999), Pat Ainley (1999), Mike Cole (1998, 1999), Richard Hatcher and Nico Hirtt (1999), Dave Hill (1999), and myself (Rikowski, 2000a-b) have indicated, New Labour's education policy is tied to a neo-liberal agenda. Basically, this agenda seeks to demolish all barriers to trade and business and the turning of all forms of enterprise (including the public sector) into capitalist ones—with production for profit and sale of products within a competitive market environment. Where the nature of the 'product' being produced makes full-blown markets difficult to institute (e.g. education, health), then forms of 'quasi-markets' are introduced (Ainley, 1999; Hill, 1999). Examples of these are internal markets in health care and funding regimes that generate competition between further education colleges, or between schools, or between schools and colleges for post-16 students (Ainley, 1999; Hill, 1999; Price, Pollock and Shaoul, 1999). Two aspects of this agenda are particularly important here. First, there is the opening up of education to business, and within a context regulated by the WTO. Secondly, there is the task of nation states to develop the labour-power within their own borders for national competitiveness in the global era. Thus, on this count, New Labour argues for the need to enhance UK labour-power for competitiveness within the context of a globalising economy.

Insofar as Seattle constituted protest against globalisation, then, by default, it challenged a New Labour strategy that is based on education and training for national competitiveness within a globalised economy. In a sense, Seattle calls the lie to New Labour's contention that there is no alternative (TINA) to bending national policies on welfare (workfare), education and training to survival in the economic maelstrom of capital's social universe. This sense of inevitability is taken a stage further by New Labour in its recent attachment to the knowledge economy (Rikowski, 2000a) and its corresponding lack of concern for the fate of the old economy. New Labour's relative lack of concern for manufacturing (witness recent events at Rover, and Ford at Dagenham), but also the old service sector (national shutdown of C&A), is the flip side of its homage to the knowledge economy.

Seattle, by implication, raised possibilities for another social universe—a social universe not *parallel* to the social universe of capital (whose substance is *value*), but a potential form of society *suppressed* within the social universe of capital: socialism, based on addressing human *need*. Seattle provided a living critique of impoverished perspectives on education resting on a taken-for-granted forwardly infinite existence of the social universe of capital. Seattle thrust the possibility of alternatives—for education, for society—before us; a lot rests on how we respond.

Peter Hudis (2000, p.1) argues that the way thousands of workers, students, feminists, gays and lesbians, environmentalists, and Third World activists came together to oppose globalisation not only raised the question of: what is the alternative to the WTO? It also raised the question of the possibility of human life beyond the social universe of capital. In turn, this puts into perspective all of the concrete social institutions comprising that social universe—including educational ones. On the other hand, new educational alternatives are springing out of the living critique of capitalism inherent in Seattle. The April edition of *News & Letters* (2000) announced that:

> As the mass protest against the World Trade Organization in Seattle show, new movements are bringing Marx's Marxism to life. His greatest work CAPITAL and his encounters with new phenomena and new movements after completing it speak to today's new stage of globalization of capitalism and the emerging revolts against it.

This is followed by an outline of five web-based classes enabling people to explore topics such as the 1992 LA Rebellion, the 1994 Chiapas uprising, What is capital? and much more—including 'Developing an alternative to global capitalism through a unity of philosophy and organization'. This is education, but not as we have usually known it[21]. It is education running against education dominated by the social production of labour-power for competitiveness in a global economy (after Cole, 1998, 1999).

Seattle has not lessened the pressure for the WTO to badger member states to dance to its tune. The WTO will be back for more on education: at national and international levels—and at the level of individual educational institutions—we must be ready for them. Through the writings of those such as Price, Pollock and Shaoul (1999), Abbie Bakan (2000a-b), Richard Hatcher and Nico Hirtt (1999, and Hirtt, 2000) the WTO's agenda for education no longer hides behind the policies of national governments.

This pamphlet has also indicated the significance of education and training for transformative and transgressive strategies; strategies seeking to move beyond existing capitalist society. Education and training are involved in producing the one commodity that generates the whole social universe of capital: labour-power. They should, therefore, play a key role in anti-capitalist movements of the future. At this point, however, it is essential to emphasise that critical, radical, Left feminist, socialist, communist, Marxist and revolutionary educators have a special responsibility to suggest alternatives to impoverished capitalist education and training—a responsibility Hillcole has taken seriously for over ten years now (Benn and Chitty, 1999). As Caroline Benn and Clyde Chitty (1999) argue, critique of existing education and training can lead to despair and low morale amongst education activists if radical alternatives are not advanced. Furthermore, radical educators have a crucial role in an educational politics of human resistance to the capitalisation of humanity through education and training. In putting forward radical alternatives, at least five considerations come into play: vision, principles, policies, critical pedagogy and organisation. This pamphlet ends with a brief discussion of each.

Vision

Paula Allman (1999) has argued that if we are to convince people of the superiority of our alternatives for education and training they must be presented with some 'vision' of what these will be like. Such visions must not be Utopias she argues, but must be grounded on the basis of existing society; they must be *realistic* alternatives. They must be alternatives that people believe can be attained. In our *Rethinking Education and Democracy* (1997) we attempted to communicate a vision of what radical alternatives in education and training would actually be like. However, argues Allman (1999), the most effective form of vision-projecting is to give people a glimpse, however brief, of the alternatives proposed. This implies a conscious, collective, open and democratic process of design and implementation of such experiments. Of course, such developments shall have to take into account resistance from the state, from some other teachers and trainers, the media and right-wing educationalists. Failure to pursue this path opens us up to the claims that our alternatives are 'impractical', Utopian and badly thought out.

Principles

Practical alternatives to capitalist education and training require underpinnings with *principles* that express different ways of learning and teaching. Hillcole has put a lot of effort into thinking through what such principles might look like and offering them up for public debate. In particular, John Clay and Mike Cole (1991) outlined some of these principles in our *Changing the Future* (Chitty, 1991). These included principles pertaining to a *socialist education policy* (which the rest of the book went on to articulate in detail). These principles were designed to address the aims of education, organisation, curriculum, democracy, post-compulsory education and popular appeal (Clay and Cole, 1991, p.9-13). Our *Rethinking Education and Democracy* (Hillcole Group, 1997) was a sustained effort in framing alternative educational principles and outlooks. More recently, Dave Hill has produced a series of papers designed to illuminate principles for progressive and socialist education (Hill, 2000a-c). These principles incorporate the more general values of social justice and equality. They set a challenge to the principles governing New Labour's education policy (exposed in Hill, 1999).

Policies
Those seeking to convince others of the need to re-design education and training for social justice, as opposed to human capital formation, have a hard time these days. The latter tends to be the centre of gravity for mainstream policy formation. Devising radical education policy is a difficult, but necessary task for the struggles ahead. In 1991, the Hillcole Group (Chitty, 1991) provided the most comprehensive set of alternative education policy proposals from the Left in the UK. The book containing these proposals, *Changing the Future* (Chitty, 1991) is still unique. Its proposals have held up well. *Changing the Future* contains education and training policies that still have relevance today. It contains critiques of existing policies (Mike Cole), proposals for changing capitalist education and training (Andy Green), new ideas on the curriculum and a critique of the National Curriculum of England (Clyde Chitty, Tamara Jakubowska, and Ken Jones), radical alternatives for teacher education (Dave Hill), proposals for education funding (Rehana Minhas and Gaby Weiner) and an outline for a New Education Act (Hillcole Group).

Critical Pedagogy
If labour-power is the weakest link in the domination of capital's rule and at the heart of socialist transformation then the question of *critical pedagogy* is crucial. How do we operate as critical educators on an everyday basis in 'really existing' capitalist schools, colleges and training organisations? The American Critical Pedagogy School is the leading movement world-wide for development of critical pedagogy. However, as Peter McLaren (2000) and Paula Allman (1999) have indicated, the problem is that American critical pedagogy has undergone degeneration as a radical alternative in the last 10 years or so. It has descended into either a 'Left' classroom technicism (e.g. obsession with seating arrangements for promoting 'the voices of all'), liberal passions abstracted from the critique of existing society and the exploration of alternatives ('critical' thinking') or the dissection of texts (the postmodern moment). Worse, radical educators such as Paulo Freire (Allman, 1999; McLaren, 2000) and Antonio Gramsci (Allman, 1999) have been domesticated in various ways. For example, Paula Allman shows how Freire's notion of

'conscientization' has been ripped apart from his overall transformative project for society. Furthermore, Peter McLaren shows how Freire's Marxist roots have either been denied or sidelined by so-called 'critical' educators in contemporary America. McLaren also demonstrates how the pedagogy of socialists such as Che Guevara has been hidden from history. Allman and McLaren call for a rethinking and rejuvenation of critical pedagogy, to make it truly *critical* once more—that is, ensure that it is linked to a project of *socialist transformation*. Mike Cole and Dave Hill have produced two edited collections that indicate, even in the harsh and tightly controlled conditions of English compulsory schooling, critical educators can still make important interventions (see Cole, Hill and Shan 1997, and Hill and Cole 1999). However, much work on critical pedagogy is required to really unsettle the dominant capitalist modes of pedagogy and their liberal education pillion riders.

Organisation

The question of organisation for the above tasks is crucial. Though the Hillcole Group has operated on most of these fronts for over ten years, certain projects call for unity and joint operations amongst Left education organisations. There is a need for solidarity against inevitable attacks from the state and other social forces as we pursue the tasks outlined above. Secondly, there is a need to consider whether some new organisations are required: an International Forum for Radical Left Educators—for the regeneration of critical pedagogy might be one such new organisation. There is a need to think creatively about the question of organisation, and how we night maximise the use of the new technologies such as the Internet—a lesson learnt by the Seattle protestors. The forces of the educational Left are relatively weak, though, we believe, growing, as New Labour's education and training policies fail to meet pre-1997 expectations and to address the general crises and tensions within capitalist education outlined in the previous section. We need to maximise our impact.

The Battle in Seattle was an inspiration to radical educators the world over. The significance of Seattle for education has been uncovered. The crucial task, however, is to convince regarding the significance of education for post-Seattle struggles, socialist transformation and an open future, a future where humanity is not dominated by capital

References

AFL-CIO (1999) *Make the Global Economy Work for Working Families—Child Labor*. At: www.aflcio.org/wto/child_labor.htm

Ainley, P. (1999) *Learning Policy: Towards the Certified Society* (Basingstoke: Macmillan).

Allen, M. (1999) Labour's business plan for teachers, in: M. Allen, C. Benn, C. Chitty, M. Cole, R. Hatcher, N. Hirtt & G. Rikowski (1999) *Business, Business, Business: New Labour's Education Policy*, A Hillcole Paper (London: Tufnell Press).

Allen, M., Benn, C., Chitty, C., Cole, C., Hatcher, R.., Hirtt, N. & Rikowski, G. (1999) *Business, Business, Business: New Labour's Education Policy*, A Hillcole Paper (London: Tufnell Press).

Allman, P. (1999) *Revolutionary Social Transformation: Democratic Hopes, Political Possibilities and Critical Education* (Westport, Connecticut & London: Bergin & Garvey).

Amsden, A. (2000) Ending Isolationism. *Dissent*, Spring: 13-16.

Antweiler, W. Jr. (1995) *A Brief History of The General Agreement On Tariffs and Trade*, at http://pacific.commerce.uba.ca/trade/GATT-rounds.html

Bakan, A. (2000a) After Seattle: the politics of the World Trade Organisation. *International Socialism*, Spring, no.86: 19-36.

Bakan, A. (2000b) From Seattle to Washington: the making of a movement. *International Socialism*, Summer, no.87: 85-93.

Balanya, B., Doherty, A., Hoedsman, O., Ma'anit, A., & Wesselius, E. (1999/2000) The World Trade Organization: 'Millennium Bug'. Corporate Europe Observatory, Amsterdam, 1999, reprinted in *Nexus*, December 1999—January 2000, 7(1): 11-16.

Beams, N. (2000) Marxist internationalism vs. the perspective of radical protest: A reply to Professor Chossudovsky's critique of globalisation, *World Socialist Web Site Review*, Journal of the World Socialist Web Site, at: www.wsws.org

Bello, W. (2000) The Iron Cage: The World Trade Organization, the Bretton Woods Institutions, and the South. *Capitalism, Nature, Socialism*, March, 11(1): 3-32.

Benn, C. & Chitty, C. (1999) Conclusion: There is an alternative, in: M. Allen, C. Benn, C. Chitty, M. Cole, R. Hatcher, N. Hirtt & G. Rikowski (1999) *Business, Business, Business: New Labour's Education Policy*, A Hillcole Paper (London: Tufnell Press).

Bristow, J. (2000) The politics of Waaaah! *LM*, February, no.127: 29.

Bright, M. (2000a) Major shake-up for state schools, *The Observer*, 11th June: 2.

Bright, M. (2000b) Sink schools: could do better, *The Observer*, 3rd September: 15.

Brokmeyer, R. (2000) Seattle anti-WTO demonstrations pose a future without capitalism. *News & Letters*, January/February 2000, at: www.newsandletters.org

Byers, S. (1999a) Speech on Globalisation by Rt. Hon Stephen Byers MP, Secretary of State for Trade and Industry to the Keidandren in Tokyo, 14th June, www.dti.gov.uk/Minspeech/byers140699.htm

Byers, S. (1999b) *Seattle Ministerial—News*. Rt. Hon Stephen Byers MP, United Kingdom Secretary of State for Trade and Industry. Address to the Opening Plenary Session of the WTO Ministerial Meeting, Seattle, 30th November 1999, at: www.dti.gov.uk/worldtrade/openspeech.htm

Callinicos, A. (1999) Inspiration from Seattle. *Socialist Worker*, 11th December: 4.

Charlton, J. (2000) Talking Seattle. *International Socialism*, Spring, no.86: 3-18.

Chitty, C. (1991) (ed.) *Changing the Future: Redprint for Education*, The Hillcole Group (London: Tufnell Press).

Chussudovsky, M. (2000) *Seattle and beyond: disarming the New World Order*, World Socialist Web Site Archive, 15th January, at: www.wsws.org

Clay, J. & Cole, M. (1991) General Principles for a Socialist Agenda in Education for the 1990s and into the 21st Century, in: C. Chitty (ed.) *Changing the Future: Redprint for Education*, The Hillcole Group (London: Tufnell Press).

Cohn, T. (2000) *Global Political Economy: Theory and Practice* (Harlow: Longman).

Cole, M. (1998) Globalisation, Modernisation and Competitiveness: a critique of the New Labour project in education, *International Studies in Sociology of Education*, 8(3): 315-332.

Cole, M. (1999) Globalisation, Modernisation and New Labour, in: M. Allen, C. Benn, C. Chitty, M. Cole, R. Hatcher, N. Hirtt & G. Rikowski (1999) *Business, Business, Business: New Labour's Education Policy*, A Hillcole Paper (London: Tufnell Press).

Cole, M., Hill, D. & Shan, S. (1997) (Eds) *Promoting Equality in Primary Schools* (London: Cassell).

De Angelis, M. (2000) Enclosure and integration, *Workers' Liberty*, no.63, July: 9-10.

DfEE (2000) Blunkett Visits China to Help Promote UK Education. *DfEE News*, 263/00, 12th June, www.dfee.gov.uk/news/

DTI (1999a) *Seattle Ministerial—News: Wednesday 1st December*. www.dti.gov.uk/worldtrade/ seattlenews.htm

DTI (1999b) *The World Trade Organisation and International Trade Rules: An Introduction to the World Trade Organisation (WTO)*. www.dti.gov.uk/worldtrade/intro.htm

DTI (1999c) *The UK and the World Trade Organisation: An Introduction to the Next Round.* www.dti.gov.uk/worldtrade/

Economist (1999a) Clueless in Seattle. *The Economist*, 4th December: 19.

Economist (1999b) The new trade war. *The Economist*, 4th December: 55-56.

Economist (1999c) The real losers. *The Economist*, 11th December: 15.

Economist (1999d) After Seattle: A global disaster. *The Economist*, 11th December: 21-22.

Elliott, M. (1999) The New Radicals. *Newsweek*, CXXXIV(24): 26-29.

Elliott, M. (1999/2000) The Risk of Losing Something Big. *Newsweek (Special Edition)*, December 1999—February 2000: 64-67.

Epstein, B. (2000) Not Your Parents' Protest. *Dissent*, Spring: 8-11.

Gleeson, B. & Low, N. (1999/2000) Annus Horribilis for Neoliberals. *Arena Journal*, no.14: 9-20.

Guardian (2000) Editorial—Protest in Prague: Opinions on globalisation are shifting, *The Guardian*, 18th September: 19.

Hatcher, R. & Hirtt, N. (1999) The business agenda behind Labour's education policy, in: M. Allen, C. Benn, C. Chitty, M. Cole, R. Hatcher, N. Hirtt & G. Rikowski, *Business, Business, Business: New Labour's Education Policy*, A Hillcole Paper, Hillcole Group of Radical Left Educators (London: Tufnell Press).

Haynes, D. (2000) Why protestors hate the free world's new mantra. *EuroBusiness*, 2(2): 36-37.

Hill, D. (1999) *New Labour and Education: Policy, Ideology and the Third Way*. A Hillcole Paper (London: Tufnell Press).

Hill, D. (2000a) *Radical Left Principles for Social and Economic Justice in Education Policy*. Paper given to the BERA Conference, 'Approaching Social Justice in Education: Theoretical Frameworks for Practical Purposes', 10th April, Nottingham Trent University.

Hill, D. (2000b) *Reclaiming our Education from the neo-liberals: Markets in Education, James Tooley, and the Struggle for Economic and Social Justice.* Paper presented at the Campaign for Free Education Conference on 'Reclaiming Our Education', University of East London, 11-12 August. (Available with an sae from the Institute for Education Policy Studies, 1 Cumberland Rd., Brighton, BN1 6SL)

Hill, D. (2000c) *Third Way in Britain: New Labour's neo-liberal education policy.* Paper presented at the European Conference on Education Research (ECER), Edinburgh, 20-23rd September.

Hill, D. & Cole, M. (1999) (Eds) *Promoting Equality in Secondary Schools* (London: Cassell).

Hillcole Group (1997) *Rethinking Education and Democracy: A Socialist Alternative for the Twenty-first Century* (London: Tufnell Press).

Hirtt, N. (2000) The 'Millennium Round' and the Liberalisation of the Education Market. *Education and Social Justice*, 2(2): 12-18.

Hines, C. (2000) Local must replace global, *New Statesman*, 18th September: 24.

Hudis, P. (2000) Can capital be controlled? *News & Letters*, April, www.newsandletters.org

Joy, B. (2000) Why the future doesn't need us, *Wired*, April: 238-279.

Klee, K. (1999) The Siege of Seattle. *Newsweek*, 13th December, CXXXIV(24): 20-25.

Lacayo, R. (1999) Rage Against the Machine. *Time*, 3rd December, 254(24): 37-41.

Lazzarato, M. (1996) Immaterial Labour, in: P. Virno & M. Hardt (Eds) *Radical Thought in Italy: A Potential Politics*, Theory Out Of Bounds, Volume 7 (Minneapolis & London: University of Minnesota Press).

Legrain, P. (2000) Against globophobia. *Prospect*, May: 30-35.

Levitas, R. (1998) *The Inclusive Society? Social Exclusion and New Labour* (Basingstoke: Macmillan).

Lowe, S. (2000) Riot Here! Riot Now! *Select*, April: 54-68.

Madden, R. (2000) If capitalism is pants, what are you wearing under your trousers? *Corporate Watch*, Spring, Issue 10: 17-19.

Madeley, J. (1999) There's a food fight in Seattle, *New Statesman Focus*, 22nd November, at: www.newstatesman.co.uk

Madeley, J. (2000) How Clare Short fails the poor. *New Statesman*, 22nd May: 23-24.

Magnussen, P. & Bernstein, A. (1999) Whose World Is It, Anyway? *Business Week*, 20th December: 34-35.

Mandel, M. & Magnussen, P. (1999) Global Growing Pains. *Business Week*, 13th December: 38-41.

Marable, M. (2000) Seattle and Beyond: Making the Connection in the 21st Century. *ZNet Update-Commentary*, 22nd January, at: www.zmag.org. Also at: www.manningmarable.net

Marshall, A. (1999) US by Third World as trade talks fail. *The Guardian*, 4th December: 16.

Marx, K. (1858) [1973] *Grundrisse: Foundations of the Critique of Political Economy (Rough Draft)*. Trans. M. Nicolaus (Harmondsworth: Penguin)

Marx, K. (1859) [1977] *A Contribution to a critique of Political Economy* (Moscow: Progress Publishers).

Marx, K. (1863) [1972] *Theories of Surplus Value—Part One* (London: Lawrence & Wishart).

Marx, K. (1866) [1976] *Results of the Immediate Process of Production*, Addendum to 'Capital', Vol.1 (Harmondsworth: Penguin).

Marx, K. (1867a) *Capital: a critique of political economy—Volume 1* (London: Lawrence & Wishart).

Marx, K. (1867b) [1977] Preface to the First German Edition of *Capital—Volume 1* (London: Lawrence & Wishart).

Mazur, J. (2000) Labor's New Internationalism. *Foreign Affairs*, January/February: 79-93.

McLaren, P. (2000) *Che Guevara, Paulo Freire, and the Pedagogy of Revolution* (Lanham, MD: Rowman & Littlefield).

Monbiot, G. (2000) Lies, trade and democracy, in: B. Gunnell & D. Timms (Eds) *After Seattle: Globalisation and its discontents*, Catalyst Book I, April (London: Catalyst Trust).

Moore, M. (1999) *Seattle: What's at Stake?* Speech to Transatlantic Business Dialogue, Berlin, 29th October, at: www.wto.org/wto/speeches/mm13.htm

MSN Encarta (2000a) *General Agreement on Tariffs and Trade*, Microsoft® Encarta® Online Encyclopedia 2000.

MSN Encarta (2000b) *World Trade Organization*, Microsoft® Encarta® Online Encyclopedia 2000.

Neary, M. & Rikowski, G.(2000) *The Speed of Life: the significance of Karl Marx's concept of socially necessary labour-time*. Paper presented at the British Sociological Association Annual Conference 2000, 'Making Time—Marking Time', University of York, 17-20th April. Forthcoming in: G. Crow & S. Heath (Eds) *Times in the Making* (London: Macmillan).

Neumann, R. (2000) A Place for Rage. *Dissent*, Spring: 89-92.

News & Letters (2000) Beyond Capitalism: The Struggle for a New Society Against Today's Globalized Capital, April, www.newsandletters.org/4.00_classes

Ovenden, K. & Bourdieu (2000) The Politics of Protest: an interview with Pierre Bourdieu. *Socialist Review*, no.242: 18-20.

Penrose, E. (1953) *Economic Planning for Peace* (Princeton, NJ: Princeton University Press).

Pontin, J. (2000) Globalization and its discontents. *Red Herring*, April, no.77: 488.
Postone, M. (1996) *Time, Labor and Social Domination: a reinterpretation of Marx's critical theory* (Cambridge: Cambridge University Press).
Price, D., Pollock, A. & Shaoul, J. (1999) How the World Trade Organisation is shaping domestic policies in health care, *The Lancet*, 354(27): 1889-1892.
Puckett, J. (2000) An Activists Dictionary for Translating WTO-Speak (Orwellian to English). *Nexus*, April—May, 7(3): 14.
Rees, J. (2000) The battle after Seattle. *Socialist Review*, January, no.237: 9.
Reese, B. (1999) Global warning. *Socialist Review*, December, no.236: 4.
Reisman, S. (1996) The Birth of a World Trading System: ITO and GATT, in: O. Kirschner (ed.) *The Bretton Woods-GATT System: Retrospect and Prospect* (Armonk, NY: Sharpe).
Rikowski, G. (1999) Education, Capital and the Transhuman, in: D. Hill, P. McLaren, M. Cole & G. Rikowski (Eds) *Postmodernism in Educational Theory: Education and the Politics of Human Resistance* (London: Tufnell Press).
Rikowski, G. (2000a) *New Labour's Knowledge Economy versus Critical pedagogy: the Battle of Seattle and its significance for education.* Paper presented at the Conference of Socialist Economists 2000, 'Global capital and Global Struggles: Strategies, Alliances, Alternatives', University of London Union, Malet Street, 1-2nd July.
Rikowski, G. (2000b) *Messing with the Explosive Commodity: school improvement, educational research and labour-power in the era of global capitalism.* Paper presented to the Symposium on 'If We Aren't Pursuing Improvement, What Are We Doing?' 7th September, Session 3.4, British Educational Research Association Conference, Cardiff University, 7th September.
Rikowski, G. (2000c) *That Other Great Class of Commodities: Repositioning Marxist Educational Theory.* Paper presented at the British Educational Research Association Conference, Cardiff University, 9th September, Session 10.21.
Rikowski, G. (2000d) The 'Which Blair' Project: Giddens, the Third Way and education, *Forum for promoting comprehensive education*, 42(1): 4-7.
Rikowski, G. (2000e) *Making Time in the UK Horological Industry Today.* Paper presented at the British Sociological Association Annual Conference 2000, 'Making Time—Marking Time', University of York, 17-20th April.
Roberts, K. (2000) Against Capitalism. *Socialism Today*, June, no.48: 2-3.
Schwartz, P. (2000) The WTO hit a speed bump in Seattle—or was it a wall? *Red Herring*, March, no.76: 96-77.
Shepherd, R. (1993) *Putting Your Finger On It: The No Problem School*, and *Once Bitten Twice Shy*, Unpublished manuscripts by Richard Shepherd, 10th March.
Short, C. (1999a) Speech by the Rt. Hon Clare Short MP. *Seattle How to make the next trade round work for the world's poor.* 29th November 1999. At: www.dfid.gov.uk/public/news/sp29nov99.html
Short, C. (1999b) What society owes the world's poor. *Folk Law*, Autumn, no.1: 3.
Short, C. (1999c) An unexpected view from a Left-wing Minister: Why a ban on child labour will not help anyone, *The Mail on Sunday*, 5th December: 26.
Short, C, (1999d) The challenge of our age. *New Statesman Focus*, 16th August, at: www.newstatesman.co.uk
Short, C. (2000) How to help the wretched of the Earth, *New Statesman*, 18th September: 22.
Smith, J. & Moran, T. (2000) WTO 101: Myths About the World Trade Organization. *Dissent*, Spring: 66-70.
Solomon, W. (2000) More Form than Substance: Press Coverage of the WTO Protests in Seattle. *Monthly Review*, May, 52(1): 12-20.
Stephens, P. (1999) Broken borders of the nation state. *Financial Times*, 3rd December: 19.

Tabb, W. (2000a) The World Trade Organization? Stop World Take Over. *Monthly Review*, January, 51(8): 1-12.

Tabb, W. (2000b) After Seattle: Understanding the Politics of Globalization. *Monthly Review*, March, 51(10): 1-18.

Thomas, M. (2000) Capital writ large, *Workers' Liberty*, no.63, July: 7-8.

Wallis, V. (2000) 2000 and Beyond: The Challenge of Capitalist Hyper-Development. *Capitalism, Nature, Socialism*, March, 11(1): 149-152.

Ward, R. & Wadsworth, R. (2000) A16, Washington DC: the battle after Seattle, *International Viewpoint*, #321, May: 4-7.

Whitfield, D. (1999) Private Finance Initiative: the commodification and marketisation of education, *Education and Social Justice*, 1(2): 2-13.

Wolf, M. (1999) In defence of global capitalism. *Financial Times*, 8th December: 29.

Working Group on the WTO/MAI (1999) *A Citizen's Guide to the World Trade Organization: everything you need to know to fight for fair trade*. Working Group on the WTO/MAI, Mobilization Against Corporate Globalization, at: www.seattle99.org

WTO (1999a) *Labour Issue is 'False Debate', Obscures Underlying Consensus, WTO Chief Michael Moore Tells Unions*. Word Trade Organisation, Press Release, press//152, 28th November, at: www.wto.org

WTO (1999b) *Seattle Conference Doomed to Succeed, Says Moore*. World Trade Organisation, Press Release, press//156, 30th November, at: www.wto.org

WTO (1999c) *'It is vital to maintain and consolidate what has already been achieved' Statement by WTO Director-General Mike Moore*. World Trade Organisation, Press Release, press release//160, 7th December, at: www.wto.org

WTO (2000) *Director-General's Press Statement*. 27th January, at: www.wto.org/speeches/mm20.htm

WTO/CTS (1998a) *Education Services: Background Note by the Secretariat*. World Trade Organisation, Council for Trade in Services, S/C/W/49, 23rd September, at: www.wto.org

WTO/CTS (1998b) *Education Services: Growth Outlook and Benefits of Liberalization*. World Trade Organisation, Council for Trade in Services, S/C/W/55, 20th October, at: www.wto.org

Zobel, G. (1999) Showdown in Seattle. *The Big Issue*, 6-12th December: 14-16.

Zynge, J. (2000) China urges speedy WTO preparations, *Financial Times*, 6th March: 13.

Notes

1   Chinese President Zhu Rongji has heralded China's entry into the WTO as indicating a 'new level of urgency in economic reform' with the relaxation of foreign investment restrictions in the country's banking, insurance, securities, telecoms and other sectors (Zynge, 2000). However, the US Congress is still required to vote to extend Normal Trading Relations (NTR) to China before gaining entry to these markets.

2   Bakan (2000a, p.24-25) indicates ten benefits listed by the WTO, p.1. The system helps promote peace; 2. Disputes are handled constructively; 3 Rules make life easier for all; 4. Freer trade cuts the costs of living; 5. It provides more choice of products and qualities; 6. Trade raises income; 7. Trade stimulates economic growth; 8. The basic principles make life more efficient; 9. Governments are shielded from lobbying; 10. The system encourages good management. Bakan (2000a) and Tabb (2000a,b) undercut many of these claims. Smith and Moran (2000) add further weight to these critiques and tackle some of the points neglected by Bakan (2000a) and Tabb (2000,a,b). They expose many of these 10 points as myths. Bello (2000) tackles points 4-9 from the perspective of how the WTO holds back development in the poor South as "Quad" interests dominate, and '... so undemocratic is the WTO that decisions are arrived at informally, via caucuses convoked in the corridors of the ministerials by the big trading powers. The formal sessions are reserved for speeches.' (Bello, 2000, p.30).

3   There are many stirring and moving eyewitness accounts on the Internet. Charlton (2000) gives a sense of what it was like to be there based on material gathered from Seattle protestors through an Internet questionnaire. The video *Showdown in Seattle: Five Days that Shook the WTO* shows the events of the week in all its brilliance—produced by Deep Dish Television for Independent Media Center and other radical organisations and for activists at www.indymedia.org, or contact *International Socialism*, PO Box 82, London E3.

4   The DTI (1999a, p.1) presented Seattle as a one day wonder, arguing that the heavier police presence after Tuesday 30th November meant that the atmosphere 'was calmer and there was no disruption of WTO activities'. Solomon (2000) demonstrates the frenzied attempts by the local, Californian and national American media to hyperspin Seattle. Klee (1999, p.2) indicates that it would be difficult for the slickest media magician to extract solace from Seattle as 'Seattle didn't feel like Earth last week—or at least not the Earth we've come to know in the peaceful and prosperous 1990s'.

5   Even Clare Short, UK Minister for Overseas Development, sensed that something special was happening in Seattle. She opined: 'I suspect that so many people have come to Seattle because they understand that history is moving under our feet' (1999a, p.1) whilst otherwise offering apologetics and misplaced hope that the WTO could reform itself in the interests of the world's poor (see Short, 1999a).

6   Bristow joins with right-wing critics of the Seattle protestors when she argues their protests merely highlighted: 'that the world is a nasty, nasty place, and it's about time the media knew about it.' For '… as a call to arms (or in this case, flowers), this is about as depressing—and pointless—as it can get. It is the politics of 'Waaaah!'—a tantrum against the general crappiness of life' (2000, p.29). This places her close to those rightists who abused the Seattle protestors as 'ignorant', spoilt middle-class people who were 'clueless in Seattle' (Economist, 1999a), having no real alternative to the world they were screaming at.

7   John Madeley (1999, 2000) points out that Short's argument that trade liberalisation 'helps the poor' falls down on the evidence. He points to a World Bank paper demonstrating that 'openness to trade is "correlated negatively" with income growth among the poorest 40 per cent of the population, but "strongly and positively" with income growth among the remaining 60 per cent' (Madeley, 2000, p.23). In particular, liberalisation of food products has destroyed jobs in farming areas in developing countries—300,000 in Sri Lanka alone, since 1996 (Madeley, 1999, p.2). Thus, trade liberalisation aids the more affluent but clearly does not 'help the poor'. A recent Editorial in *The Guardian* (Guardian, 2000) cited a World Bank report published in the second week of September 2000 that economic growth does not necessarily reduce poverty and that inequality is bad for growth. Secondly, another report from the Performance and Innovation Unit (of the UK Cabinet Office) acknowledges that 'there are serious environmental costs to trade liberalisation' (*ibid.*).

8   As Elliott indicated, amongst those who stressed the importance of globalisation many positions were advanced. A key point was that '… one of the most important lessons of Seattle is that there are now two visions of globalization on offer, one led by commerce, one by social activism' (Elliott, 1999, p.28).

9   At the extreme, this perspective readily links up with some strands of communitarian thought that ultimately have conservative and pro-capitalist implications. Ruth Levitas (1998) provides a timely warning against viewing Seattle as the basis for re-building "community" within capitalist social relations (see her chapter 5, 'Community Rules' in particular).

10   The main thrust of Neumann's argument is against violence as a tactic. There was a substantial Internet debate post-Seattle regarding whether violence was legitimate for the cause of anti-capitalism. In particular, there were many discussions on the politics and ethics of trashing Starbucks and other houses of consumer capitalism.

11   As Madeley (2000) shows, Clare Short's positions on the WTO (it can be reformed) trade liberalisation and globalisation (they can be good for the poor if they have more of a voice in

reformed institutions such as the WTO), together with other statements Short has made on child labour, indicate that she comes close to supporting the continuance of child labour, or at the least has a shoulder-shrugging attitude. There is little to choose between Short and *The Economist* that argued that: 'Neither trade, nor globalisation in general, would be sufficient to give that Indian child [on the front cover] a better life. Above all she needs education, and health, and much else. But without trade, and the faster growth it can bring, she is unlikely to get any of it' (Economist, 1999c, p.15).

12   See Ovenden and Bourdieu (2000)—on the situation in France.

13   For a thorough analysis of New Labour's business agenda for education see Allen *et al* (1999), and in particular Hatcher and Hirtt (in Allen *et al*). Hatcher and Hirtt's analysis of what is going on in education in the UK and in the EU generally shows how current education policies of EU nations and the educational agenda of the WTO (privatisation of education provision and liberalisation of education services) fit snugly together.

14   Such as the Private Finance Initiative (PFI). Whitfield (1999) explores the PFI in relation to education.

15   This section owes a lot to two papers presented at the British Educational Research Association Conference 2000, Cardiff University, 7-9th September (Rikowski, 2000b-c).

16   Marx had made this point earlier in *A Contribution to a Critique of Political Economy* (1859, p.27) and also in the *Grundrisse* (1858, p.881).

17   See also: 'The commodity is, first of all, an external object, a thing which through its qualities, satisfies human need of whatever kind (Marx, 1858, p.125).

18   As Martin Allen (1999) indicates, the processes involved have a dual aspect: on the one hand schools are being redesigned to business goals, and on the other they are being recast as business organisations. His analysis focuses largely on the second aspect. This is complemented by Mike Cole's (1999) analysis of the first aspect.

19   Of course, the private sector has made much bigger inroads into areas of education other than in the direct running of schools 'at the chalkface'- in providing payroll and human resource systems, consultancies, as recruitment agencies, as purveyors of IT systems, security systems, school meals, cleaning and so on.

20   See Rikowski (1999, p.60-62) on workers selling their labour-powers (not *themselves*) to capital for a fixed duration in return for a wage, making them 'wage slaves' rather than slaves in the classical Greco-Roman sense (where the *whole person* is sold and duration is unspecified, maybe unto death).

21   See www.newsandletters.org/4.00_classes.htm.

Post-Nice Postscript

> I do not understand what they are protesting about and it would be a complete failure of leadership if we were to give in to the protestors. (UK Prime Minister Tony Blair, at the EU Nice Summit, in an article by Stephen Castle, *The Independent*, 8th December, 2000)

> What will the students who were protesting at the World Trade Organization in Seattle do once they graduate? Cynics expect that their activist ideals will slip away as they grab the first job that offers stock options. By contrast, 36 out of 40 students I interviewed said they plan to join social justice, labor or environmental-rights organizations in the United States and abroad. (Bhumika Muchhala, *Student Movement Is Thriving After Seattle*, 2000a, p.1-2)

Early drafts of this pamphlet generated considerable discussion within the Hillcole Group. At the centre of this discussion was the decision to include material from the writings of Karl Marx and to use this as a resource for developing a perspective on the strategic significance of education for post-Seattle anti-capitalist struggles. Whilst some within the Hillcole Group saw nothing wrong with this (and indeed supported this move), other members advanced a number of objections to some aspects of the content, the style or mode of presentation. In resolution, it should be noted, therefore, that not all members of the Hillcole Group share all of the views expressed within this pamphlet.

Meanwhile, the anti-capitalist struggle continues. I write two days after the protest in Nice against the EU Summit. At the Summit meeting, Tony Blair was set to argue against the Charter of Fundamental Rights for EU citizens. One of the 52 articles of the Charter proclaims that people are entitled to education, health and welfare. The Charter also declares that workers can defend their interests by resorting to strike action, thus calling into question UK industrial relations law where no such positive *rights* exist (Castle, 2000). On the other hand, the UK Government's support for GATS continues. As Hilary Wainwright notes:

> The year 2000 is to be brought to a close by the opening round of the auctioning of selected public services to the world's most predatory—mainly US—corporations. This process is sanctioned by GATS (the General Agreement on Trade in Services), and items that could be on offer range from Mexico's telecommunications to Britain's schools. (2000)

Wainwright points out that there has been no real discussion in the British parliament about GATS. In the US, it was Ralph Nader who raised the issue before the US electorate. The *Financial Times* (2000) indicated recently that the WTO was picking itself up after its disaster in Seattle a year ago and is in the process of reformulating a new trade round, with all the implications for the privatisation of education uncovered in this pamphlet. Gibby Zobel writes:

> Only this week [27th November–3rd December] the European Services Forum, a powerful lobby group of 50 multi-nationals and 36 trade federations, will meet to discuss the cutting up of public services across the world for the profit of their shareholders, regardless of individual government wishes. The UK is legally bound to sell them off, as signatories to the 1994 WTO agreement. (2000, p.23)

Consolidated opposition to this process is necessary, agues Zobel.

Many struggles call the lie to the notion that we just have to put up with the world as designed by the triad (WTO, IMF and World Bank) and the corporations they represent and nurture. For example, Ana Dinerstein's (2000) remarkable paper shows how the unemployed, poor and dispossessed, workers (with support from trade unions), children and owners of small and medium-sized businesses (p. 5) in Argentina have struggled against the IMF's 'adjustment programme' for their country. Their response has been dramatic, incorporating a *new form of resistance*, argues Dinerstein: *roadblocks*. The latest wave of roadblocks was during April and May, 2000. Bonfires were made in the middle of roads (often out of old tyres), guarded by pickets. For example:

> On the 2nd of May, nearly 3,000 inhabitants of General Mosconi blocked the motorway leading to Bolivia by means of two barricades, pickets and a bonfire made of burning tyres. Three hundred men, armed with slingshots, stick, stones and some Molotov cocktails, firmly prevented any movement. (Dinerstein, 2000, p.p. 5)

Dinerstein argues that the roadblocks, as a novel and effective method of resistance, were crucial in generating the confidence of Argentina's workers to call a general strike for 9th June. The support for the strike was massive (p. 9). Furthermore, argues Dinerstein, the roadblocks 'allow the redefinition of identities, the expansion of solidarity networks and new forms of organisation and resistance' (p.11). Most of all, they 'manifest the struggle for the recognition of the centrality of *labour* in capitalist society' (p.13—my emphasis).

There is always an alternative. Regarding opposition to the take-over of our schools by private corporations, we need to show the same degree of courage and creativity as the Argentinian roadblockers reported on by Dinerstein. Radical educators have a responsibility to work with others in generating new visions beyond capitalist education and training and to struggle for alternatives to social life as currently constituted. As Paula Allman (2001a, p.13) argues:

> ... we must not fear being ridiculed for our critical utopianism or for trying to ignite the fire of hope in people's hearts and minds. For some, that fire may have been extinguished. Instead, they profess or have succumbed to an utterly ludicrous utopia—the one that arises from the belief that liberal democracy can continue to buffer us from the worst excesses of capitalism, and the equally ridiculous and dangerous belief that it can enable us to continue to live as civilised beings regardless of the deepening and expanding of capital's contradictions, which inevitably accompanies their displacement into the global arena.

Radical educators must seek to offer alternatives and to give these organisational forms through 'cross-border alliances with teachers, with working men and women, and with social movements collectively dedicated to smashing capital's rule' (McLaren, 2000, p.8). On this score, argues Peter McLaren:

> We continue to fight because we must, not because we are assured of victory. The mere chance of victory is reason enough. (*ibid.*)

Radical Left educators seek to maximise the chances of victory for a society where social justice is possible (Rikowski, 2000) and education and training are linked to need and not profit-generation.

The pamphlet ends where it began, with Seattle. The following are excerpts from Bhumika Muchhala's *Student Voices: One Year After Seattle* (Muchhala, 2000b). I urge all readers of this pamphlet to read also Muchhala's incredible text. Muchhala interviewed student activists who were at Seattle, one year after the Battle in Seattle:

> So much of our education is being squandered in random distractions or used in the pursuit of material wealth in this society where it's not enough to fill the human spirit. (Irene Jay Liu, junior at Yale University, New Haven City Council candidate)

As I was marching in Seattle, I watched 2000 people coming down one street. I turned around and saw another crowd of people marching behind me. Seeing the two crowds merging on the intersection with so much energy was an amazing experience for me, because I know that the three months of organizing work I had put in had helped create that sight. (Emily Reilly-Burg, sophomore at Mills College, organizer for the National Student Encounter in Defense of Education in Seattle, Washington)

During the WTO protests, we were marching up one hill where there were cops lined across the entire street. People inside buildings were peering out of their windows. Looking at the front of the march, there seemed to be many people going up the hill, but when I turned around and saw thousands of people coming up behind us, everything suddenly hit me—the power of our voices and the enormity of what we were doing. (Carlos Marentes, senior at Seattle Central Community College, organizer for the National Student Encounter in Defense of Education in Seattle, Washington)

I now question what is being taught in school, why some things are being taught and not others. Understanding those things that are not taught in school is at the core of confronting our capitalist system, in which the roots of our race and economic problems lie (Jerome Chavez, 5th year student at the University of New Mexico, 180 MDE co-ordinator)

Jerome's final statement applies to radical teachers and educators too, for:

This is a light that always burns in some hearts, somewhere; the task is to enable it to burn more brightly and widely until it obliterates the horizon of capitalism. (Paula Allman, 2001b—in press)

Glenn Rikowski
London, 10th December 2000

References

Allman, P. (2001a) Education on Fire! In: M. Cole, D. Hill, G. Rikowski & P. McLaren, *Red Chalk: On Schooling, Capitalism & Politics* (Brighton: the Institute for Education Policy Studies).

Allman, P. (2001b) *Critical Education Against Global Capital: Karl Marx and Revolutionary Critical Education*. In press (Westport, Connecticut & London: Bergin & Garvey).

Castle, S. (2000) Amid the clouds of tear gas, a disparate alliance is united in protest. *The Independent*, 8th December: 3.

Dinerstein, A. (2000) *Roadblock in Argentina: fighting virtual disappearance*. Unpublished paper, Department of Sociology, University of Warwick. A version of this paper is forthcoming in *Capital & Class*, journal of the Conference of Socialist Economists.

Financial Times (2000) Trade Agenda (Editorial). *Financial Times*, 8th December: 22.

McLaren, P. (2001) Gang of Five, in: M. Cole, D. Hill, G. Rikowski & P. McLaren, *Red Chalk: On Schooling, Capitalism & Politics* (Brighton: the Institute for Education Policy Studies).

Muchhala, B. (2000a) Student Movement Is Thriving After Seattle. *Corporate Watch*, at: www.corpwatch.org/feature/wto/8-youth. html Originally in the *Boulder Daily Camera*, 25th November 2000.

Muchhala, B. (2000b) *Student Voices: One Year After Seattle*. Institute for Policy Studies, 733, 15th Street, NW, #1020, Washington, DC 20005, at: www.ips-dc. org

Rikowski, G. (2000) *Education and Social Justice within the Social Universe of Capital*. Paper presented at the British Educational Research Association Day Seminar on 'Approaching Social Justice in Education: Theoretical Framework for Practical Purposes', Faculty of Education, Nottingham Trent University, 10th April. Available from Education-*line*, at www.leeds.ac.uk/educol/documents/00001618

Wainwright, H. (2000) We need to be guerrillas. *The Guardian*, 5th December: 23.

Zobel, G. (2000) The whole world in their hands. *The Big Issue*, November 27—December 3, no. 414: 22-23.

56

Business, Business, Business
New Labour's Education Policy
Martin Allen, Caroline Benn, Clyde Chitty, Mike Cole,
Richard Hatcher, Nico Hirtt, Glenn Rikowski

The three chapters in this pamphlet explore New Labour's business agenda for education.

Chapter 1 unearths the roots of 'New Labour's education outlook: globalisation, competitiveness, and modernisation, revealing its weaknesses and the consequences of this approach. Chapter 2 argues that Labour's business agenda for education is not unique. Education throughout the EU is being restructured to accommodate the interests of big business in the 'new era' of globalisation, and the consequences of this agenda are explored. In chapter 3, Martin Allen pursues the issue of what business incorporation of schooling means for teachers.

In the conclusion, Caroline Benn and Clyde Chitty argue that the left must go beyond critique of existing policy drives and construct an education policy in which the values and goals of democracy, equality and real educational and social progress are central.

ISBN 1 872767 915   paperback   £3.00

New Labour and Education:
Policy, Ideology and the Third Way

Dave Hill

Dave Hill identifies 45 elements of New Labour's education policy, and places them on an ideological spectrum from centre-left to post-Thatcherite. Is Labour's education ideology inchoate and contradictory—a mixture of ideologies? Or does its much vaunted policy priority of 'education, education, education' represent the triumph of Thatcherism, subservient to the interests of 'business, business, business'? While some of the terminology may be specific to Britain, the analysis of New Labour's education policy here can inform judgements about their overall ideological trajectory and about similar Third Way policies in other states.

ISBN 1 872767 869   paperback   £3.00

Rethinking education and democracy: A socialist alternative for the twenty first century

co-ordinated by Caroline Benn *and* Clyde Chitty for
the Hillcole Group

The twenty-first century will need an education system very different from that of today.
In this book the Hillcole Group takes up the challenge of thinking the truly thinkable to describe a vision of an education system based on principles of equality and democratic accountability to take us into the new millennium. We must move beyond the 30 year war of weak social democratic pragmatism and rigid conservative dogmatism and their inadequate and unsuccessful solutions for education. Education is for people of all ages, it is a fundamental part of life, not a preparation for it.

We provide the framework for an alternative education based in a society which itself must be changed from the constraints of past thinking into a culture of social entitlement. We apply these principles, drawing out the transformative implications for all levels of education in the current system. Our aim is to provide a radical vision of what education and society could be like in the twenty-first century.

ISBN 1 872767 45 1   *paperback*   £7.95

Changing the future: Redprint for Education

The Hillcole Group edited by Clyde Chitty

Even Adam Smith said that education was too important to leave to the whim of the market place, and we must reassert the social principles on which education should be based, for the good of the individual and society. The future that the free market ideologists plan for us must be changed.

In this book the Hillcole Group renew and extend their criticism of changes made to and proposed for the education system. They move beyond criticism to outline their proposals for an integrated comprehensive education-training system, from pre-school to post-18 and beyond, based on principles of equality and democratic accountability. Changes are proposed for the structure of the system, for curriculum and assessment, for teacher education, and for resources and funding. The proposals are drawn together in a New Education Act which provides an educational charter for the entire population, integrating education and training throughout the system. New bodies would be established to monitor and enforce high standards of participation, achievement and provision at all stages, and to integrate preparation for work with education for personal and community development. The Hillcole Group have laid down a challenge to all political parties, and revitalised the 'Education Debate' with a fresh vision of the future for education.

ISBN 1 872767 25 7   paperback   £8.95

Equal Opportunities in the new ERA
Ann Marie Davies, Janet Holland & Rehana Minhas
The authors examine the implications of the 1990 Education Reform Act and the National Curriculum for equal opportunities in relation to gender, race and class.
ISBN 1 872767 30 3   Paperback   £3.95

Something Old, Something New, Something Borrowed, Something Blue: Schooling, Teacher Education and the Radical Right in Britain and the USA
Dave Hill
Dave Hill examines Radical Right attacks on liberal-democratic and social-egalitarian models of schooling and teacher education in Britain and the USA.
ISBN 1 872767 05 2   Paperback   £3.95

Training Turns to Enterprise: Vocational Education in the Market Place
Pat Ainley
Pat Ainley reviews the phases of education policy since the war and describes the reviews of vocational qualifications seeing in 'access' and modularisation the future direction of many education reforms.
ISBN 1 872767 10 9   Paperback   £3.95

Markets, Morality and Equality in Education
Stephen Ball
Stephen Ball explores the political and ideological antecedents of the education market established by the 1990 Education Reform Act.
ISBN 1 872767 15 X   Paperback   £3.95

What's left in teacher education: Teacher education, the radical left and policy proposals
Dave Hill
Hill makes a series of challenging proposals for a Labour Government to enact. He promotes the concept of the teacher as a critical reflective practitioner.
ISBN 1 872767 20 6   Paperback   £3.95

Whose Teachers? — A radical manifesto
Hillcole Group
Teacher education from the 1990s has been under pressure. The Hillcole Group presents alternative proposals offering a democratic vision of teacher education which is critical in the project of developing professional teachers for children and the future.
ISBN 1 872767 40 0   Paperback   £3.00

Red Chalk:

On Schooling, Capitalism and Politics

Mike Cole, Dave Hill, Peter McLaren and Glenn Rikowski

...Our collective idea was that this booklet would enable us to start a dialogue about educational reform by situating the political project that animates our lives in our lived experience as educational activists...

...Dave, Mike, Glenn, and Paula have, in distinctly creative ways, used Marxist theory to re-direct current educational debates in the theatre of educational critique.

Peter McLaren (University of California, Los Angeles, USA)

...this exciting conversation amongst four of the world's most committed and significant critical/radical educators. This publication (which began as an interview but reads much more like a conversation or discussion) demonstrates poignantly that education has the potential to fuel the flames of resistance to global capitalism, as well as the passion for socialist transformation.

Paula Allman (Nottingham University, UK)

...Red Chalk was an exciting read... I was moved by the form of it, the debate, the concerns...

Kevin Harris (Macquarie University, NSW, Australia)

ISBN 0-9522042-0-5   paperback   £7 plus 50p p&p from
INSTITUTE *for* EDUCATION POLICY STUDIES
1 Cumberland Rd.
Brighton BN1 6SL UK

www.ieps.org.uk

Postmodernism in Educational Theory:
Education and the Politics of Human Resistance
edited by Dave Hill, Peter McLaren, Mike Cole and Glenn Rikowski

Postmodernism has become the orthodoxy in educational theory, particularly in feminist educational theory. It heralds the end of grand theories like Marxism and liberalism, scorning any notion of a united feminist challenge to patriarchy, of united anti-racist struggle and of united working-class movements against capitalist exploitation and oppression. For postmodernists, the world is fragmented, history is ended, and all struggles are local and particularistic.

Written by leading and internationally renowned British and North American socialist and Marxist thinkers and activists, Postmodernism in Educational Theory poses a serious challenge to this postmodern orthodoxy. Authors critically examine the infusion of postmodernism and theories of postmodernity into educational theory, policy and research. In addition, issues such as social class, 'race' and racism, gender, education policy and policy analysis, youth, and capital and commodification are addressed.

Writers in the book argue that despite the claims of self-styled 'postmodernists of resistance', postmodernism provides neither a viable educational politics, nor a foundation for effective radical educational practice. In place of postmodernism, the book outlines a 'politics of human resistance' which puts the challenge to capital(ism) and its attendant inequalities firmly on the agenda of educational theory, politics and practice.

ISBN 1 872767 818   *paperback 233pp*   £15.00